# SPEAKING CHRISTIAN

# SPEAKING CHRISTIAN

Why Christian Words Have Lost
Their Meaning and Power—And
How They Can Be Restored

## MARCUS J. BORG

HarperOne
*An Imprint of* HarperCollins*Publishers*

HarperOne

HarperCollins books may be purchased for educational, business, or sales promotional use. For information, please e-mail the Special Markets Department at SPsales@harpercollins.com.

HarperCollins website: http://www.harpercollins.com

HarperCollins®, ✤®, and HarperOne™ are
trademarks of HarperCollins Publishers

FIRST HARPERCOLLINS PAPERBACK EDITION PUBLISHED IN 2012

Library of Congress Cataloging-in-Publication Data
Borg, Marcus J.
Speaking Christian : why Christian words have lost their meaning and
power—and how they can be restored / Marcus J. Borg.
p. cm.
ISBN 978–0–06–197658–2
1. Christianity—Terminology. 2. Theology. 3. Language and languages—
Religious aspects—Christianity. I. Title.
BR96.5.B67    2012
230—dc23                                                                    2011044578

14  15  16  17  18    RRD (C)    12  11  10  9  8  7  6  5  4  3

To my sister Beverly, who died in March 2010, soon after her eightieth birthday. She was my "big sister," twelve years older than I, a second mother, I suspect, when I was a baby and toddler, and throughout our lives together a best friend.

# Contents

## Contents

# Introduction

Christian language has become a stumbling block in our time. Much of its basic vocabulary is seriously misunderstood by Christians and non-Christians alike. Big words like *salvation, saved, sacrifice, redeemer, redemption, righteousness, repentance, mercy, sin, forgiveness, born again, second coming, God, Jesus,* and *Bible* and collections of words like *the creeds, Lord's Prayer,* and *liturgies* have acquired meanings that are serious distortions of their biblical and traditional meanings.

The misunderstandings flow from two major causes shaping the way Christian language is heard. The first is the literalization of language in the modern period, affecting Christians and non-Christians alike. The second is the interpretation of Christian language within a common framework that I call "heaven and hell" Christianity, which I describe more fully in Chapter 1. When this is the primary framework for understanding Christianity, as it often is, it diminishes and distorts the meaning of Christian language.

Christians in this country (and elsewhere) are deeply divided by different understandings of a shared language. About half (maybe more) of American Christians believe that biblical language is to be understood literally within a heaven-and-hell framework that emphasizes the afterlife, sin and forgiveness, Jesus dying for our sins, and believing. The other half (maybe less) puzzle over and have problems with this. Some have moved on to another understanding of Christian language. The differences are so sharp that they virtually produce two different religions, both using the same Bible and the same language.

This book's purpose is to exposit an alternative understanding, one that draws on the Bible and premodern Christian tradition. It has a drumbeat. Again and again, it compares and contrasts the contemporary meanings of Christian language with their often very different biblical and traditional meanings. Again and·again, it names the effects that literalization and the heaven-and-hell framework have had upon the meanings of Christian language. Again and again, it reveals the more ancient and authentic meanings of "speaking Christian" and tries to connect these reinvigorated meanings to the realities we face in the twenty-first century.

The book's purpose is to redeem or reclaim Christian language in all of its richness and wisdom. Indeed, I had thought of titling the book *Redeeming Christian Language,* but then I realized that *redeeming* is one of the words that need redeeming. Today it is usually associated with being redeemed from our sins by the death of Jesus, our Redeemer. However, its more ancient and biblical meaning works very well. To *redeem* means to set free from slavery, bondage, captivity; it is not about being saved from our sins. In this sense, Christian language needs to be redeemed—to be set free from its captivity to contemporary literalism and the heaven-and-hell Christian framework.

Because I have written books about Jesus, God, the Bible, and the heart of Christianity, some repetition of topics treated in them is inevitable. However, when I do treat material in this book that I have presented before, the exposition is fresh as well as more concise.

The chapters are of varying lengths. Some are as long as traditional book chapters. Others are only two or three pages. The deciding factor was how much exposition was needed to clarify the topic of the chapter.

This book might also be seen as "a Christian primer." A primer teaches us how to read. Reading is not just about learning to recognize and pronounce words, but also about how to hear and understand them. This book's purpose is to help us to read, hear, and inwardly digest Christian language without preconceived understandings getting in the way. It is about learning to read and hear the language of our faith again.

# CHAPTER I

# Speaking Christian

S peaking Christian," by which I mean knowing and understanding Christian language, is in a state of crisis in North
America. I suspect the crisis extends to other parts of the
world as well, but I write about the cultural terrain I know best.
The crisis is twofold. For many, an increasing number, Christianity has become an unfamiliar language. Many people either do not
know the words at all or, if they have heard the words, have no idea
what they mean.

But Christian illiteracy is only the first part of the crisis. Even
more seriously, even for those who think they speak "Christian"
fluently, the faith itself is often misunderstood and distorted by
many to whom it is seemingly very familiar. They think they are
speaking the language as it has always been understood, but what
they mean by the words and concepts is so different from what
these things have meant historically, that they would have trouble
communicating with the very authors of the past they honor.

So why do I express this crisis as a problem of language? Because language is the medium through which people participate in
their religion. To be part of a religion means being able to speak
and understand its language. Every religion has a basic vocabulary:

its "big" words and collections of words, spoken and heard in worship, embodied in rituals and practices.

Thus to be Jewish means "speaking Jewish"; to be Muslim means "speaking Muslim"; to be Buddhist means "speaking Buddhist"; and so forth. By "speaking" I do not mean merely knowing either the ancient languages of these religions or their modern descendants. I mean something more basic: the way practitioners use the concepts and ideas from their religion as a lens through which to see the world, the way they use them to connect their religion to their life in the world.

To use an illuminating phrase from recent scholarship, religions are "cultural-linguistic traditions."[1] What this means is both simple and important. Every religion originated in a particular culture and thus used the language of that culture, even if in ways that radically challenged it. If a religion survived over time, it became a cultural-linguistic tradition in its own right, with its own language, its basic vocabulary, sacred texts and stories, rituals and practices. These are often organized into comprehensive systems of thought—what Christians call theology, including doctrines and dogmas.

In this respect, being Christian (or Jewish or Muslim) is like being French (or Turkish or Korean). One of the criteria for being French is the ability to speak French. Another is being able to understand French. We would not think someone fluent in French if that person could only speak it, but not understand it. In the same way, literacy means more than simply being able to make sounds out of written words. It also involves having some understanding of what the words mean. Christian literacy means not simply the ability to recognize biblical and Christian words, but also to understand them.

Of course, being Christian is about more than words, just as being French is about more than fluency in French. One doesn't become French simply by learning the language. Being French also involves membership in a community and an "ethos," a way of life. So also being Christian is about being part of a community and an ethos, a way of life. It is about more than language, but not less.

Christian language is grounded in the Bible and postbiblical Christianity. It includes the words used, heard, sung, and prayed in worship, devotion, teaching, and community. To be Christian is to know, use, and be shaped by this language—to live one's life with God within the framework of this language.

## An Unfamiliar and Misunderstood Language

Christian language is becoming unfamiliar for an obvious reason. Over the last half century, the percentage of people growing up Christian has decreased significantly in North America and even more so in Europe. Many born after the mid-1960s have had little exposure to biblical and Christian language, except what they may have picked up from a culture in which Christianity is a strong presence.

I became vividly aware of this shift thirty years ago when I moved from teaching in Minnesota, where Christian language was in the air that we breathed, to teaching in Oregon, the least churched state in the country. On the first day of my first class, an introduction to the New Testament, I said that we couldn't understand the New Testament without understanding that early Christianity was rooted in Judaism. A hand went up: "What's Judaism?"

Good question. What is a one- to five-minute response to somebody who doesn't know anything about Judaism and wants to know what it is? As I sought to define Judaism, I mentioned Moses, and another hand went up: "Who's Moses?" Another good question. How do you say who Moses was to somebody who has never heard of him?

I knew that I wasn't in Minnesota anymore. Many of my students in Oregon had little familiarity with the Bible and Christianity. I began to ask them on the first day of courses to write a ten-minute essay on the topic "Me and the Bible" or "Me and Christianity." Some questions they had to answer were: What has been your exposure to Christianity and the Bible? Did you grow up in a church? And whether you did or not, what have you heard about the Bible and Christianity? What's your impression?

Here is a sampling of what I read and learned:

"I don't know much about the Bible, but I think there's a story in it about a guy in a fish."

"I don't know much about Christianity, but I think that Christians are really against trespassing."

Half had never been to a church service, except for a wedding or funeral, and not all had experienced even that.

More than half described Christians as literalistic, anti-intellectual, judgmental, self-righteous, and bigoted.

One who had never been to a Christian worship service happened to attend what may have been the only snake-handling church in Oregon. He said that he hadn't known that Christian worship included snakes, and he thought that was pretty interesting.

The problem wasn't the intelligence of my students; they were bright. But they were harbingers of a future that is becoming more and more present. Many Americans under forty have grown up with little or no involvement in a church. Of those born since 1980, 25 percent describe themselves as having no religious affiliation.

Unfamiliarity with Christian language—its important words and the sacred texts and stories in which those words are embedded—is widespread among Christians as well. Polls indicate that less than half of American Christians can name the four Gospels. Only a third know that the Sermon on the Mount is in Matthew. Two-thirds think that the saying "God helps those who help themselves" comes from the Bible (it doesn't). Most know only a few stories from the Old Testament, often in garbled form. Stories from the New Testament fared only slightly better. Thus, even for many Christians the language of the Bible and Christianity is like a foreign language.

The problem is not simply unfamiliarity. Many of us have heard Christian language since childhood. If we are still part of a church, we continue to hear it in biblical readings, sermons, hymns, prayers, liturgies, and creeds. We are steeped in it.

The problem is that it is often misunderstood. It has acquired meanings that are very different from their biblical and ancient meanings. Sometimes the issue is diminishment, the reduction of rich and multiple meanings to one particular meaning. Often the issue is even more serious, not just diminishment, but distortion and serious misunderstanding.

There are two major reasons why the Christian language is frequently misunderstood today. First, a particular common and widely shared understanding of what Christianity is has created a framework within which biblical and Christian language is most often understood. I call it the heaven-and-hell framework. The second reason we misunderstand Christian terms is the result of the "literalization" of biblical and Christian language. This is my name for the process by which many have come to assume that the most faithful way to understand Christian terms is as literal and absolute representations of the inerrant revelation of God. In this chapter, we will tackle the heaven-and-hell framework and take up the literalization of Christian language in the next chapter.

## THE HEAVEN-AND-HELL FRAMEWORK

Words have their meanings within frameworks. Frameworks are large interpretive contexts that shape the meanings of words. *Elephant* means something very different in the framework of a visit to a game park in Africa from what it means in the framework of a political cartoon. Frameworks matter.

The large framework shaping the meaning of Christian language for many today is the heaven-and-hell Christianity of not so long ago. I have puzzled, indeed struggled, with what to call this, seeking to avoid terms that sound pejorative or patronizing, yet still wanting to use ones that give an accurate description. By *heaven-and-hell Christianity,* I mean simply an understanding of Christianity that most Protestants and Catholics shared in common and thus took for granted not very long ago.

Suppose that you had been asked at the end of childhood, at age twelve or so, the following questions: What is Christianity about? What is the heart of its message, "the gospel"? Why should people be Christian? The questions are relevant not only for those who grew up Christian. Virtually everybody who grew up in a Western culture acquired some impression of Christianity by the end of childhood.

At that age, my single-sentence answer, the impression that formed in my mind as I grew up Christian a half century ago, would have been: Jesus died for our sins so that we can be forgiven and go to heaven, if we believe in him. Of course, I learned that being Christian was about more than that. It also meant seeking to lead a changed life by obeying God's commandments, especially the commandment to love one another. It was about behavior as well as belief. But its core was clear. We have been bad and deserve to be punished, even to the extent of eternal torment in hell. But God sent Jesus to die for us so that, if we believe in him, we can be forgiven and go to heaven.

This understanding was not idiosyncratic to my Scandinavian Lutheran childhood. Rather, it was widely shared by Protestants and Catholics. With varying degrees of conviction, it continues to be seen as the core of Christianity by millions, within and outside the church. It is the framework within which many understand Christian language.

The heaven-and-hell framework has four central elements: the afterlife, sin and forgiveness, Jesus's dying for our sins, and believing. They are all there in my childhood memory and present in the minds of many Christians. What is already in our minds shapes what we experience, including how we hear words.

*The Afterlife:* Heaven is the reason for being Christian. Life after death was so important in the form of Christianity that I absorbed growing up that if somebody had convinced me when I was twelve or so that there was no afterlife, I would have had no idea what Christianity was about or why I should be Christian.

This is the understanding held by many Christians today. Some belong to churches that explicitly emphasize the hope of heaven and the threat of hell. Others belong to churches that seldom or never mention hell. But even for many of them, the hope of a blessed afterlife is what Christianity is most centrally about. How important has the promise of heaven (and perhaps the threat of hell) been to the forms of Christianity that you have experienced or heard about?

*Sin and Forgiveness:* Sin is the central issue in our life with God. Forgiveness is the solution. Because we are sinners, we deserve to be punished. Consider how often sin and forgiveness appear in Christian worship. Most services include a confession of sin. In my childhood, every Sunday morning we said, "We poor sinners confess unto thee that we are by nature sinful and unclean, and that we have sinned against thee by thought, word, and deed, wherefore we flee for refuge to thine infinite mercy, seeking and imploring thy grace, for the sake of our Lord Jesus Christ." That's pretty intense, though not as severe as some I have heard. Confessing sins wasn't just Protestant; my Catholic friends had to go to confession every Saturday and confess in person to a priest.

Most worship services also include a threefold appeal for God's mercy: "Lord, have mercy upon us. Christ, have mercy upon us. Lord, have mercy upon us." We need God's mercy because we are sinners. The words of the Eucharist (also known as the Lord's Supper, Mass, or Communion) commonly emphasize our sinfulness and Jesus as the sacrifice who makes forgiveness possible. Take time to reflect on how central sin and forgiveness were to your impression of Christianity.

That heaven-and-hell Christianity is "sin-ridden" is often more apparent to non-Christians than Christians. Some years ago I heard a Buddhist teacher say with a twinkle in his eye, "You Christians must be very bad people—you're always confessing your sins and asking for forgiveness."

*Jesus Died for Our Sins:* Within this framework, what is most important about Jesus is his death. He died for our sins in our place, paid the price of our disobedience, and thereby made our forgiveness possible. This understanding is widespread not only among the many who affirm it, but also among many who have misgivings about it or reject it.

Recall Mel Gibson's blockbuster movie *The Passion of the Christ*. It focused on the last twelve hours of Jesus's life, from his arrest through his torture, suffering, and death, and portrayed all of this as Jesus's bearing the sins of the world. Recall its enthusiastic reception by many conservative Christians. Even Pope John Paul II endorsed it; he said, "It is as it was." The message was clear that what matters most about Jesus is his death as a substitutionary sacrifice for the sins of the world.

The connection between an afterlife and Jesus dying for our sins is insisted upon by conservative Christian voices in America today. For example, Albert Mohler, president of the flagship Southern Baptist Theological Seminary, said in 2010: "Did Jesus go to the cross as a mere victim? If so, then we have no gospel, we have no hope of everlasting life. Did Jesus go merely as a political prisoner, executed because he had offended the regime? Well, if so, that's a very interesting chapter of human history, but I'm not going to stake my life on it, much less my hope for eternity."[2]

Note how his statement combines the "gospel," the "hope of everlasting life," and the "hope for eternity" with Jesus being more than "a mere victim," more than "a political prisoner executed because he had offended the regime." For Mohler and many Christians, what matters about Jesus is that he died for our sins, so that we can be forgiven and go to heaven.

*Believing:* The final element that makes up the heaven-and-hell framework is believing, understood as affirming a core set of statements to be true. Believing, or "having faith," is what God wants from us and what makes it possible to go to heaven. For about half of Protestants, this means not only believing that Jesus died for our sins, but much more, including that the Bible is the inerrant revelation of God, literally and absolutely true. For other Protestants and most Catholics, what is to be believed is not as rigorously detailed. But there is common agreement that affirming a set of beliefs matters. For many, this has become the primary meaning of "faith."

The framework created by these four elements decisively shapes the meaning of many "big" Christian words, giving them meanings very different from their biblical and ancient Christian ones. To illustrate:

*Salvation* now refers to life after death; it is about going to heaven. But in the Bible, it is seldom about an afterlife; rather, it is about transformation this side of death.

*Saved* now means to be saved from our sins. But in the Bible, it is about much more than this, and often not about sin at all.

*Savior* now refers to Jesus as the one who saves us from our sins. But in the Bible, *savior* is used long before Jesus and most often has nothing to do with being saved from sin.

*Sacrifice* now refers to Jesus's death on the cross as payment for our sins. But in the Bible, sacrifice is never about substitutionary payment for sin.

*God* now refers to a personlike being separate from the universe. God's character is both loving and punitive. God loves us enough to send Jesus to die for us, but God will also judge and punish those who don't believe or behave as they ought. But the Bible also contains a very different understanding of God, both of what the word refers to and of God's character.

*Mercy* is now about God forgiving us, even though we are sinful and deserve to be punished. But in the Bible, the ancient words translated into English as *mercy* often do not mean what *mercy* means in modern English.

*Repentance* is now remorse for sin and resolving to live a better life. But in the Bible, its meanings are quite different: to return from exile and "to go beyond the mind we have."

*Redeemer, redeem,* and *redemption* (like *savior, save,* and *salvation*) now refer to Jesus as the redeemer who redeems us from our sins and brings about our redemption. But in the Bible, these words are not about being saved from sin, but about being set free from slavery.

*Righteousness* is now primarily about individual virtue—about being a righteous person. But in the Bible, it is often a collective or social virtue. It is about justice and whether societies are just or unjust.

*Peace* is now primarily understood as an individual internal state—peace of mind and being at peace with God. But in the Bible, peace is more than internal peace. It is a major part of God's dream for the world, a world of nonviolence and the end of war.

*Faith* now means believing a set of statements about God, Jesus, and the Bible to be true, often literally true. But in the Bible and premodern Christianity, faith and believing are not about affirming the truth of statements. Rather, they are about commitment, loyalty, and allegiance, and not to a set of statements, but to God as known especially in Jesus. Perhaps the best single synonym for *to believe* is *to belove.*

All of these words and more will be treated in this book. For now, the point is that the common heaven-and-hell framework is like a black hole that sucks the meaning of Christian language into it, changing and distorting it.

Because much of this book is a critique of how this framework has narrowed and distorted the meaning of much of Christian language, I want to emphasize that it has worked and still works for millions. By *worked,* I mean that it had good effects in their lives.

My own parents, born over a century ago, are an example. I think they and many in their generation lived within the framework of conventional heaven-and-hell Christianity all their lives. So far as I know, it didn't create problems for them—though I wish I had thought to ask them while they were still alive. In part, it worked for them because it was taken for granted and was thus "softer" than its hardened contemporary forms. It didn't require willed affirmation and vigorous defense. For them and for many, it was a means of grace whereby the Spirit of God worked in them, producing the fruits of gentleness, decency, and compassion. God's Spirit can and does work through many means.

But in our time, the meaning of Christian language within the heaven-and-hell framework of conventional Christianity has become a problem for many. For some, it renders much of Christian language opaque and deprives it of its richness. For others, the issue is more than deprivation; Christian language has become an obstacle, an intellectual stumbling block, sometimes so large that taking Christianity seriously becomes very difficult.

## Redeem or Replace?

So serious is the problem that some have concluded that Christian language is beyond redemption and needs to be replaced by language that actually communicates what we want to communicate. If *salvation* means something very different from what most people think it means, can we use the word without being misunderstood? If *God* means something very different from what it means to most people, can we use the word without being misunderstood? So also with many others, like *saved, mercy, righteousness, repentance,* and so forth.

A powerful case for the need to replace Christian language is made by Gretta Vosper, a pastor in the United Church of Canada, president of the Canadian Center for Progressive Christianity and author of *With or Without God: Why the Way We Live Is More Important Than What We Believe.*[3] She invites her readers to imagine what a visitor to a typical mainline worship service experiences:

> Readings from the Bible that are not only unfamiliar, but sometimes disturbing, concluding with "The Word of the Lord," followed by "Thanks be to God."
>
> Prayers that presuppose that God can be persuaded to intervene.

A liturgy that emphasizes that we have been sinful, but Jesus paid the price by dying for us.

Language about bread and wine as the body and blood of Jesus given for us.

What does this language mean to outsiders, or, for that matter, to insiders, to Christians? Vosper's book makes a bracing case for changing our language that needs to be taken seriously by all who are concerned with the viability of Christian language today.

But I choose the second option, to redeem rather than replace Christian language. One reason is personal. As an Episcopalian, I belong to a denomination saturated with Christian language. Every Sunday, we hear four biblical readings, more than most other Christians do. Our liturgies and prayers from the Book of Common Prayer are filled with biblical and Christian language. For me to abandon this language would mean leaving a biblical and liturgical denomination that has been and is profoundly nourishing.

The second reason is more than personal. It is the premise of this book that religions are like languages. If we take this seriously, it means that being Christian means speaking Christian. To cease to speak Christian would mean no longer being Christian—just as ceasing to speak French would mean no longer being French. Speaking Christian is essential to being Christian.

I do not want to be misunderstood. People can live a good life without knowing or using Christian language. And by "a good life" I do not mean simply a happy life or decent life, but a transformed life that embodies virtues enshrined in Christianity. Christianity is not the only path of goodness and transformation. But

Christianity has repeatedly shown itself throughout its history to be an effective path for goodness and transformation—a path that is affirmed by millions and still has the potential to be a powerful force for our future. That is why I think it is worth redeeming rather than replacing Christian language. We have too much to lose.

What it means to redeem Christian language is illuminated by the primary biblical meaning of *redeem:* to set free, to release from bondage. Christian language needs to be set free, released, reclaimed from its captivity to its conventional modern meanings.

Redeeming Christian language includes reclaiming individual words and short phrases like *salvation, saved, sacrifice, redemption, repentance; God, Jesus, Trinity; righteousness, mercy, justice, grace, the kingdom of God; eternal life; Jesus* as *Lord* and *Savior,* as *the Way and the Truth and the Life,* and more. We need to ask afresh: What does this language mean? What does it means to use these words? It also means redeeming collections of words heard in Christian worship: biblical readings, the Lord's Prayer, creeds, the liturgy, especially the Eucharist.

The language of the Bible and postbiblical Christianity is much richer and broader than commonly supposed. The latter includes language used by saints, mystics, and theologians like Augustine, Thomas Aquinas, Francis of Assisi, Julian of Norwich, Catherine of Sienna, Teresa of Avila, John of the Cross, Martin Luther, John Calvin, and many others. The tradition also includes the imaginative enhancement of Christian language in Christian art, music, hymnody, and poetry.

Thoughtfully understood, Christian language is perceptive, persuasive, and powerful. Its insights about the human condition illuminate the way we commonly experience our lives. It points to an alternative vision and way of life centered in God and God's passion for a different kind of world. It has power. For many it has been and continues to be a sacrament of the sacred, a means of grace, a way the Spirit of God speaks to us, a vehicle whereby our lives are changed. But how we understand this language matters.

# CHAPTER 2

# Beyond Literalism

The second reason Christian language has become a problem for millions today is the modern church's embrace of literalism as the most faithful way for understanding its key terms and language. Although a literal-factual understanding of language is widespread in the modern world, it is actually a recent development, the product of the last few centuries. For many, Christians and non-Christians alike, the literalization of language is at work in the heaven-and-hell framework within which Christian language is often understood.

Biblical literalism typically goes hand in hand with an understanding of the Bible as the inerrant and infallible revelation of God. About half of American Protestants belong to churches that teach this. Like Christians in general, they affirm that the Bible is the "Word of God" and inspired by the Holy Spirit. But they draw a particular inference that distinguishes them from other Protestants as well as from Catholic and Orthodox Christians. They infer that because the Bible is the inspired Word of God, it is inerrant and infallible.

Here is the logic they use. A perfect God would not inspire an imperfect Bible. The inspiration of the Bible gives it a divine guarantee of being true—literally, factually, and absolutely. If the

Bible says something happened, it happened. If it says something is wrong, it's wrong.

The impact upon Christian language, on the meaning of "speaking Christian," is immense. Christians who think the Bible is inerrant and to be interpreted literally and absolutely also commonly do the following:

They affirm that the earth and the universe are less than ten thousand years old. Why? Because, figuring backward from our time, a literal reading of the early chapters of Genesis and biblical genealogies yields about six thousand years. Some even specify the year of creation as 4004 BCE. Thus they oppose evolution, since its long time span contradicts the Bible's young age of the earth and our descent from a literal Adam and Eve. For them, the conflict between religion and science is an enormous issue. They ask themselves: Are we to believe in God and the Bible or in science?

They affirm that the stories of spectacular events in the Bible really happened: the flood in the time of Noah; the ten plagues and the sea dividing in two in the story of the exodus; the virginal conception of Jesus; Jesus's healings, walking on water, multiplying loaves, and so forth; and his bodily resurrection. God really did wondrous things in ancient times. In the minds of these Christians, it's important, indeed crucial, that these events really happened—or else the Bible and Christianity aren't true.

They commonly oppose gender equality. Wives are to be submissive to their husbands, and women are not to be clergy. Why? Because the Bible contains some passages that teach the subordination of women and prohibit them from having authority over men.

They see same-sex relationships as sinful. Why? Because the Bible contains a few passages that condemn such relationships.

They insist that Jesus is the only way of salvation and that Christianity therefore is the only true religion. Only people who believe in Jesus can be saved. Why? Because a few passages in the New Testament say so.

These examples reflect a "hard" form of literalism that insists on the inerrant and absolute truth of biblical language. It is the most visible form of American Christianity today, proclaimed in fundamentalist and most conservative-evangelical denominations and in most megachurches. It dominates Christian television, radio, and the Christian political right.

A "softer" form of literalism extends to other Christians beyond those who affirm literalism in its hard form. This softer form was common in the recent Christian past among both mainline Protestants and Catholics.

My experience growing up Lutheran fifty years ago is somewhat typical. We learned that the Bible is the "Word of God" and "inspired by God." What this meant to me (and most of us, I think) was that the Bible came from God as no other book does. This is what gave the Bible its authority; because it originated in God, it is God's revelation. We took it for granted that it was the final authority for faith and morals. It told us what to believe and how to live.

Yet we were not committed to biblical inerrancy and biblical literalism. We knew that some Christians thought that, but we didn't. We didn't insist on a literal reading of the creation stories in Genesis, and so we didn't have to choose between the Bible and evolution. We had no difficulty extending the six days of creation into geological epochs. I never had to wonder how dinosaurs fit into the picture. And it was okay—even if a bit daring—to think that the story of Jonah living for three days in the belly of a fish was a parable and not a factual story.

But we did take it for granted that the really important events happened more or less as described. So we also accepted the fact that the Bible's teachings about morality came from God and told us how to live. If the Bible said something was wrong, that pretty much settled the question.

"Soft literalism" continues to operate in the minds of some within mainline denominations today, as illustrated especially by the conflict about the status of gays and lesbians. If the Bible says homosexual behavior is wrong, does that settle it? Are the Bible's teachings about sexuality the absolute revelation of God? If so, then changing Christian teaching on same-sex relationships is impossible. But if not, then what does biblical authority mean? This question—the authority of the Bible and how to hear its language—is at the center of this conflict. Is the Bible to be understood as the literal and absolute revelation of God?

## INERRANCY AND LITERALISM AS MODERN, NOT ANCIENT

Because many Christians think that biblical inerrancy and its literal-factual-absolute interpretation are traditional and orthodox, it is important to know that this is not so. Rather, this understanding of Christian language is recent, the product of the past few centuries.

The factual inerrancy of the Bible was first explicitly affirmed just over three centuries ago in the second half of the 1600s in a book of Protestant theology. The claim was a reaction to the Enlightenment, that period of Western cultural history that began not long before with the birth of modern science and scientific ways of knowing—with figures like Copernicus in the 1500s, Galileo in the early 1600s, and Newton later in that century. Also commonly known as "modernity," the Enlightenment has decisively shaped contemporary thinking. For many in our time, Christians and non-Christians alike, it has led to an identification of truth with factuality. The effects upon the understanding of language are far-reaching, because according to this view either statements are factually true or they aren't true at all.

Though biblical inerrancy and literalism emerged within Protestantism, they went beyond what the major figures of the Protestant Reformation of the sixteenth century thought. True, the Reformers did emphatically affirm biblical authority. Scripture was the source and the ground of their courage as they stood against the religious and imperial authorities who ruled their world. *Sola scriptura*—"The Bible alone"—was foundational for Martin Luther's theology. It became a battle cry of the Reformation.

But Luther and the other Reformers did not affirm inerrancy or literalism. Luther thought that both James and Revelation should be thrown out of the New Testament. To say the obvious, you cannot think this and also think of the Bible as the inerrant revelation of God.

Nor was Luther a literalist. Consider his interpretation of the story of Adam and Eve in Eden. In Genesis 3:8 we read that after Adam and Eve had eaten the forbidden fruit, they heard the sound of God walking in the garden and were afraid. Luther commented that God obviously never walked in any garden. Something else is meant. Adam and Eve heard the sound of the wind and nature, which formerly had seemed benign, but now, because of their fallen state, had become something they were afraid of.

Inerrancy and literalism are not part of the origins of Protestantism. Indeed, as a widespread understanding among Protestants, insistent or hard literalism is much later than its first affirmation in the 1600s. Its roots are really in the late 1800s and early 1900s.

The impact of literalism on Christian language makes the Bible and Christianity incredible for many. It is a major reason that many young people have little or no interest in Christianity. Though some are enthusiastic members of churches that proclaim biblical inerrancy and literalism, the majority find these ideas literally unbelievable. They cannot see how one particular religion is the only true religion or that its language must be interpreted literally and absolutely.

But literalism is not only a public relations problem that needs to be addressed for the sake of outsiders. It also very much affects insiders; for Christians, it narrows, reduces, flattens, and ultimately distorts the meanings of the Bible and Christianity.

## A Historical-Metaphorical Understanding

Mainstream biblical scholarship provides an alternative way of understanding Christian language that is richer and fuller and does not create the intellectual stumbling blocks generated by literalism. Like literalism, it is a recent development, the product of the last few centuries. But its roots are ancient, going back to the Bible itself. Though shared by mainstream biblical and theological scholars, it does not have a commonly agreed-upon shorthand name. To give it one, I call it a *historical-metaphorical approach*.

A historical approach to biblical and Christian language means something simple and important, but is also sometimes misunderstood. To begin with the possible misunderstanding, one of the meanings of *historical* in contemporary English concerns factuality. When presented with a surprising story about the past, we sometimes ask, "Is that historical?" and we mean, "Did it really happen?" A historical approach to the Bible can ask that question and can sometimes make reasonably informed probability judgments about an answer. But that is not what I mean by *historical*.

Rather, a historical approach means setting biblical and Christian language in their ancient historical contexts. What did these words mean in and for the ancient communities that used them? What did they mean for their "then"? For example, a historical approach asks the following:

The six-day story of creation in Genesis was probably written during or after the Jewish exile in Babylon in the sixth century BCE. What did it mean in that setting?

Most of the prophets of ancient Israel spoke in the eighth through sixth centuries BCE. What did their words mean in the context of what was happening in Israel in those centuries?

The book of Deuteronomy was probably written in the seventh century BCE. How does what was happening in the life of ancient Israel then help us to understand the book?

What did *salvation* (and *saved* and *savior*) mean for ancient Israel? In the story of the exodus? In the experience of exile in Babylon? In the book of Psalms, the prayers and hymns of ancient Israel? In the first century, the time of Jesus and the emergence of the early Christian movement?

What did words like *Lord, Son of God, Messiah, Savior, sacrifice,* and so forth mean before they were applied to Jesus? What did they mean when they were applied to Jesus by his early followers?

What did the language used in the Nicene Creed mean to those who created it in 325 CE?

What did the word *person* mean to those who formulated the doctrine of the Trinity—one God in three persons—in the fourth century CE?

A historical approach is greatly illuminating. Language comes alive in its context. Moreover, a historical approach prevents us from projecting modern and often misleading meanings back into the past. It is a way of escaping the provinciality of the present. It recognizes that the Bible was not written to us or for us, but within and for ancient communities.

Thus a historical approach makes Christian language relative and not absolute. For some Christians, this is threatening. For them, the word *relative* has only a negative meaning. It means "not important" or even "not true," as when people say dismissively, "It's all relative." But *relative* also has a positive meaning—it means "related to." In this sense, *relative* means, "This is how our spiritual ancestors saw things." Their language, the language of the Bible and the postbiblical Christian tradition, is related to their time and place, *their then.*

To recognize that biblical and Christian language is relative does not mean that it has no important meaning for our time.

But it does change the question. The question is no longer simply, "What does the Bible say?" as if that would settle everything. Rather, the question becomes, "Given what their words meant for *their then,* what might their meaning be for *our now*?"

For example, both the Old Testament and the New Testament contain regulations that concern slavery. The regulations are about their time and place, their then. But do they hold the same meaning for our now? Until at least the Civil War, many American Christians thought so, in the North as well as the South. But there arose other Christians who felt that other, more general principles taught by scripture (about equality, love, justice, human dignity, and so on) made the slavery passages of their then no longer applicable to our now. Today, I don't know any Christians who think we should reestablish slavery, because passages in the Bible say it's all right. Christians have rightly relativized that teaching, recognizing it as being about their then (and maybe even wrong in their then).

When we see the meanings of biblical and postbiblical Christian language for their time and place, we see their "relatedness." Understanding is enriched, not impoverished. What it means for our now needs to take into account how they saw things then. But what it meant for their then may not be what it means for our now.

The second adjective in the *historical-metaphorical approach* takes seriously that language, especially religious language, often has a more-than-literal, more-than-factual, more-than-historical meaning. This is its metaphorical meaning. Metaphor is about "the surplus of meaning" that language can carry.[1] Metaphorical meaning is not inferior to literal-factual meaning—it is not less than, but more than.

The justification for a metaphorical approach is found in the Bible itself. Much of its language is overtly metaphorical. For example, it speaks of God as a *rock*. What is the literal meaning of that? Obviously, God is not a rock. The Bible speaks of the *right hand of God*. What is the literal meaning of that? God does not have hands. Something else, something more, is meant. This is the metaphorical meaning.

Approximate synonyms for metaphorical meaning are *symbolic* and *parabolic*. Symbolic language points beyond itself; its meanings are not literal or factual. So also parabolic language. Consider the parables of Jesus. No Christian I know insists that they are factual—that, for example, there really was a good Samaritan or a prodigal son, and that Jesus was just reporting something that happened the other day. Rather, Jesus made these stories up. Their point is their meaning, not their factuality.

A metaphorical approach to biblical and Christian language emphasizes meaning, not literal factuality. In this sense, the purpose of most biblical stories is metaphorical, even if they sometimes contain historical memory. Why did ancient Israel preserve and tell the stories and traditions that they did? Because they saw them as having a more-than-literal significance that continued into their present.

Consider the account of beginnings in Genesis. The universe, earth, and life are created in six days. Then Adam and Eve in the Garden of Eden are tempted by a talking serpent to eat the forbidden fruit and are expelled from paradise into a world of suffering, to life "east of Eden." Biblical literalism affirms that the tellers of these stories were reporting "what happened," that there really was an Adam and Eve and a Garden of Eden and a talking snake a long time ago. But is that what these stories are about?

From antiquity, biblical and Christian theologians have seen these stories as a profound metaphorical portrayal of the human condition and of our radical dependence upon God. Their surplus of meaning is minimally twofold: that we and the whole of creation have our origin in God; and that although we begin our lives in the presence of God, something has gone wrong, and we live our lives east of Eden and yearn to return.

Consider the story of Israel's exodus from slavery in Egypt. It dominates the first five books of the Bible and is the foundation of the Bible as a whole. The story includes:

The rescue of the infant Moses from the death decree of Pharaoh;

The voice of God speaking to Moses from a fiery bush that burned without being consumed;

The ten plagues that God sent upon Egypt;

The parting of the sea and the destruction of Pharaoh's army as it pursued the freed slaves;

The giving of the commandments to Moses on Mt. Sinai;

Miracles of nourishment in the desert—water from rocks, manna and quail falling from the sky, the latter sometimes covering the ground three feet deep (imagine getting up in the morning and having to shovel your way through the quail);

Violent divine punishments because of idolatry during the forty years in the wilderness.

Biblical literalism affirms that these are factual reports about the past, about spectacular things God did back then, including divine violence. But is that what these stories are about?

Aren't their surplus meanings, their more-than-factual meanings, really the more important ones? According to a metaphorical interpretation, the exodus is about the human condition as marked by bondage to the lords who rule this world, and about God's passion that we be liberated from bondage and embark on a journey that leads from Egypt to the promised land.

In the New Testament, consider the stories that early Christian communities told about Jesus. Why did they tell these stories? Simply because they wanted to report what happened? Or was it because of the surplus of meaning, because they saw the more important purpose of these stories—that they had meaning for their lives?

For example, in John, Jesus heals a blind man who then exclaims, "Though I was blind, now I see" (9:25). Is the primary purpose of this story that a spectacular healing happened in the past, that Jesus healed a person born blind? Or is the point that Jesus is the "light of the world" (9:5) for all people? Or, further, is the point that the story amplifies words from the first chapter of John, how Jesus is the "true light" who "enlightens everyone" (1:9)?

To think that "Though I was blind, now I see" is just an exclamation on the occasion of a great and perhaps unrepeatable event that happened once upon a time long ago misses its meaning. Rather, as the hymn "Amazing Grace" puts it, the story's language applies beyond its time: "I once was blind, but now I see." "Seeing" is not primarily the regaining of physical sight. It is when metaphorically blind people have their eyes opened. This is the story's surplus of meaning, its more-than-factual meaning, its metaphorical, symbolic, parabolic meaning.

Biblical and Christian language is rich. It needs to be redeemed from its cultural captivity to literalism. When understood literally and absolutely, it becomes incredible. For many, Christian faith becomes believing in the literal and absolute truth of statements that you otherwise wouldn't take seriously. But is that what being Christian is? Is that what the God of the Bible and Jesus want from us? Is that what will save us? Or do we need an exodus from the bondage of literalism? Does "Let my people go" apply now just as it did then?

For Christians who affirm biblical inerrancy and literalism, letting go of it can be frightening and unsettling, for it means letting go of certainties. For many other Christians, it has been an experience of liberation.

# CHAPTER 3

# Salvation

W e begin our exploration of specific Christian words with *salvation*. I do so partly because of its importance and partly because it provides an especially clear case study of the distortion of the meaning of Christian language by the heaven-and-hell framework described in Chapter 1.

To say the obvious, *salvation* is a very big Christian word. It names the yearning, desire, hope, and purpose of the Christian life. It is as central to Christianity as *nirvana* and *satori* (enlightenment) are to Hinduism and Buddhism. Thus what we think *salvation* means matters greatly.

*Salvation* is a loaded word. It carries a lot of baggage for many people. I have been aware of this for a long time, but I was nevertheless struck by the strength of its negative associations in an intergenerational discussion group that I recently facilitated. Half were in their twenties and thirties, and half in their sixties and seventies. Most were committed and intentional Christians involved in their churches. The rest were earnest seekers—no longer or not yet part of a church, but seriously considering whether there might be something real and important in Christianity.

For 80 percent of the group, *salvation* had *only* negative associations. These went back to childhood and teenage years. Salvation was about going to heaven. Though that might sound appealing, the opposite possibility—going to hell—was deeply alarming. For those raised in fire-and-brimstone churches, the threat of hell was explicit. Most had experienced a softer form in which hell was seldom if ever emphasized—but the possibility of hell was still there in the language they heard in church.

Salvation as "going to heaven" affected their understanding of its sibling terms *saved* and *savior*. Because the obstacle to going to heaven was sin, to be *saved* meant being saved from their sins. *Savior* referred to Jesus dying for their sins in order to make their salvation possible. What they needed to do was to believe in Jesus and repent of their sins.

They recalled, even as children, worrying about whether they had believed and behaved as they needed to in order to be saved. Salvation was laden with anxiety, subsumed as it was within a fear-based Christianity. For some, the threat of hell had been used in emotionally abusive and manipulative ways to control their behavior. Many of these left the church, often for decades; resentment and rejection replaced fear.

Most also reported being bothered by the exclusiveness that went with this understanding of salvation. They were told, or absorbed, that only Christians could be saved—that is, go to heaven. And often only the right kind of Christians would go to heaven, which meant Christians like them. Others did not remember that this was emphasized, but heard biblical language that seemed to say so, especially the "one way" passage in the Gospel of John: "I am the way, and the truth, and the life. No one comes to the Father except through me" (14:6). Salvation was associated with a sharp division between those who were saved, who were "in," and those who were not. Many recalled at least a whiff of righteousness in their churches about being in the "in" group, while most of the world was not. As one reported, "Salvation and smugness go together."

These understandings became unpersuasive at different points in their lives—for some it was in their teens, for others it was later. Only Christians can go to heaven? We are saved from our sins by Jesus as a blood sacrifice? Jesus's death was God's plan of salvation—God sent Jesus to be killed, to die in our place as payment for sin? Only people who believe this can be saved? Really? Is that the way things are?

## CONTEMPORARY MEANINGS

Their understanding of salvation as "going to heaven" reflects its most common meaning in modern English. A recent poll asked respondents if they agreed or disagreed with the statement, "Many religions can lead to eternal life."[1] As the poll explained the statement, it equated "eternal life" and "eternal salvation" with "going to heaven," thereby presupposing this is the purpose not only of Christianity, but of religions in general.

The connection between salvation and being saved from our sins by the death of Jesus is also widespread in modern English. Consider these definitions from three contemporary dictionaries.[2] Keep in mind that the purpose of dictionaries is not to define "truth," but to describe common usage—what words most commonly mean.

*American Heritage: Salvation* in a Christian context is
"deliverance from the power or penalty of sin; redemption."
*Redemption* is then defined as "salvation from sin through
Jesus's sacrifice." *Save* is defined as "to set free from the
consequences of sin: redeem."

*Random House Webster's: Salvation* means "deliverance from
the power and penalty of sin; redemption."

*Oxford American: Salvation* means "deliverance from sin and
its consequences, believed by Christians to be brought about by
faith in Christ."

The biblical meanings of *salvation, saved,* and *savior* are very different, richer, and much more comprehensive than these dictionary
definitions. To see this, we need to pay attention to how frameworks shape meaning. Just as their common meanings have been
shaped by the framework of sin, forgiveness, and heaven, their
biblical meanings are shaped by frameworks.

Within their biblical frameworks, these words are about much
more than sin and forgiveness, heaven and hell. They speak about
the transformation of life this side of death—about personal transformation and political transformation. They are about the transformation of our lives as individuals and as people living together
in societies.

## BIBLICAL MEANINGS

*Salvation* and its siblings appear almost 500 times in the New Re-
vised Standard Version of the Bible (NRSV), the Bible most widely
used in mainline Protestant churches today.[3] *Salvation* occurs 127

times; *save, saved, saves,* and *saving,* about 300 times; *savior,* about 40 times. Roughly two-thirds are in the Old Testament and the rest in the New Testament.

Because *salvation* in common usage is closely associated with "going to heaven," we need to clear up a major misunderstanding at the outset. *Salvation in the Bible is seldom about an afterlife.*

In the Old Testament, for almost all of the centuries it covers, the people of ancient Israel did not believe in an afterlife. The concept appears nowhere in the stories of the ancestors in Genesis or the exodus from Egypt, nowhere in the passionate words of the prophets or the praise, prayers, and wisdom of Psalms, Proverbs, Ecclesiastes, and Job. The first clear reference to life beyond death is in Daniel, chronologically the last book in the Old Testament to be written, about 165 BCE.[4] Even there, *salvation* is not used to speak about an afterlife. Salvation, as we will see, was about something else.

In the New Testament, *salvation* is occasionally about an afterlife—but most of the time it is not. So also *saved* and *savior* are not primarily about being saved from our sins so that we can go to heaven. In both the Old and New Testaments, the primary meanings of these three words are very different from their common modern meanings.

As we turn now to biblical texts in which these words appear, imagine that you don't know what they mean. Let their meanings be shaped by the biblical contexts, the biblical frameworks, within which they are used. Our interpretation of these texts uses the historical-metaphorical approach sketched in Chapter 2.

*Salvation as Liberation from Bondage:* The first biblical framework shaping the meaning of salvation is the story of the exodus from Egypt. Set in the thirteenth century BCE, it tells the story of the Israelites' enslavement to Pharaoh, the political, economic, and religious lord of their world. Then God, through the leadership of Moses, liberates them from bondage. The story includes their entry into a new way of life together, beginning with the covenant with God at Mt. Sinai, continuing on the long journey through the wilderness, and ending with them about to enter the promised land.

This story is the ancient Israelites' "primal narrative," the most important story they knew and foundational to their understanding of God and life with God.[5] Remembered and celebrated every year at Passover, it is to the Old Testament and Judaism what the story of Jesus is to the New Testament and Christianity.

*Salvation* and *saved* appear at one of the dramatic high points of this story of liberation from bondage. As the fleeing slaves are trapped between Pharaoh's army and the sea, facing death or reenslavement, God makes a path through the sea, the Israelites pass through, and the sea rushes back and drowns the forces of Pharaoh. Then the author of Exodus says, "Thus the LORD *saved* Israel that day from the Egyptians" (14:30). A hymn celebrates the deliverance: "The LORD is my strength and my might, and God has become my *salvation*" (15:2).

In Israel's memory of the exodus in the prophets and Psalms, *savior* is used. In Hosea 13:4, God says: "I have been the LORD your God ever since the land of Egypt; you know no God but me, and besides me there is no *savior*." In Psalm 106:21, God is "their *Savior,* who had done great things in Egypt."

Within the framework of the exodus, note how comprehensive the meanings of *salvation, saved,* and *savior* are. Salvation involves *liberation from economic bondage:* the slaves in Egypt were exploited and impoverished, condemned to unremitting hard labor, and given only meager rations. *Liberation from political bondage:* in

Egypt, they had no power, no voice, no say in how the system was put together. *Liberation from religious bondage:* Pharaoh would not give them permission to worship their God, whose passion was for a different kind of world.

Salvation as liberation from these forms of bondage shaped the life of ancient Israel. Consider the radical economic laws found in the Torah, the Pentateuch. No interest was to be charged on loans. Every seventh year, all debts were to be forgiven, and those who had fallen into indentured slavery because of debt were to be set free. Every half century (the jubilee year), the ownership of all agricultural land was to be returned to the original family without compensation. The intent of these laws was to prevent the emergence of a permanently impoverished underclass. The Israelites had been saved from Egypt, and Egypt was not to be re-created in Israel.

In the first centuries after the exodus, the ancient Israelites had no king. Why? Because in Egypt they had experienced the oppression and exploitation that went with kingship. When kingship did emerge in Israel around the year 1000, some protested that a king would be a new Pharaoh.[6] Israel was to have no other king, no other lord, than the one who had brought them out of Egypt. The absence of kingship was not about radical individualism or anarchy; Israel was a corporate entity, a people called to live life together in accord with the covenant with God.

So also the exodus story and the meaning of salvation within it were foundational for the prophets of the Old Testament. In the centuries after the rise of kingship, prophets such as Amos, Isaiah, Micah, Jeremiah, and others indicted the monarchy as a new Pharaoh responsible for re-creating Egypt within Israel—a system of political and economic oppression that denied the God of Israel, who had liberated them, or *saved* them, from Egypt.

*Salvation as Return from Exile:* The second major framework shaping the biblical meaning of salvation is the Jewish experience of exile in the sixth century BCE. It began when the Babylonians conquered and destroyed Jerusalem and took many of the survivors into exile in Babylon. There, like their ancestors in Egypt centuries earlier, they were oppressed, impoverished, and powerless. The exile lasted for about fifty years and ended when Persia conquered Babylon and the Persian emperor Cyrus decreed that the exiles could return to their homeland.

This is the historical context for the second part of the book of Isaiah, beginning with chapter 40. Its magnificent language is familiar to millions because of Handel's *Messiah*. Consider how these phrases from the oratorio come alive in the historical setting of exile and return:

"'Comfort ye, comfort ye, my people,' saith your God." These opening words of Isaiah 40 deliver a message of consolation and are followed by the proclamation that Israel's time of suffering is over.

"The voice of him that crieth in the wilderness, 'Prepare ye the way of the Lord.'" A way—"the way of the Lord"—is being prepared for the exiles to return.

"Every valley shall be exalted, and every mountain and hill made low, the crooked straight, and the rough places plain." God is building a highway, an interstate, an *Autobahn* in the desert that separates Babylon from the homeland.

"He shall feed his flock like a shepherd." As they journey through the wilderness, God will care for them as a shepherd cares for the flock.

In this context of exile and return, the second part of Isaiah abounds with the words *salvation, saved,* and *savior.* The first two are combined in Isaiah 45:17: "Israel is *saved* by the LORD with everlasting *salvation.*" Half of the occurrences of *savior* in the Old Testament are in this part of Isaiah. One occurs near the end of this glorious passage:

> But now thus says the LORD. . . . Do not fear . . . I have
> called you by name, you are mine. When you pass through
> the waters, I will be with you; and through the rivers, they
> shall not overwhelm you; when you walk through fire, you
> shall not be burned, and the flame shall not consume you.
> For I am the LORD your God, the Holy One of Israel, your
> *Savior.* . . . You are precious in my sight, and honored, and I
> love you. . . . Do not fear, for I am with you. (43:1–4)

Note how God as *Savior* is associated with:

God's presence on the journey: when you pass thorough waters, rivers, fire, flame, "I will be with you."

God's love: "I have called you by name, you are mine. . . . You are precious in my sight, and honored, and I love you."

God's assurance: "Do not fear"—twice, both in the context of God's presence.

All of this—release from Babylon, a journey of return, God's presence and love—is the meaning of *savior, salvation,* and *saved.* Salvation is return from exile—coming home.

*Salvation as Rescue from Peril:* Rescue is the primary meaning of salvation in the Psalms. The longest book in the Bible, it is a collection of prayers, hymns, and liturgies—the worship and prayer book of ancient Israel. The Psalms tell us how our spiritual ancestors praised God, invoked God, and prayed to God.

*Salvation* appears in the Psalms more often than in any book in the Bible, including those in the New Testament. It is mostly about rescue, deliverance from peril and danger. Sometimes it is individual deliverance and sometimes collective deliverance—of the people, the nation. Sometimes the peril is illness. Often the peril is posed by enemies or "the wicked." Sometimes the petition is to be saved from death, "the Pit"—but this is not about surviving death and entering into a blessed afterlife. Rather, this is being saved from a potentially mortal illness or from enemies who desire the death of the petitioner(s).

A sampling of passages from the Psalms that use salvation and its siblings:

The LORD is my light and my salvation; whom shall I fear? (27:1)

Restore to me the joy of your salvation. (51:12)

By awesome deeds you answer us with deliverance, O God of our salvation. (65:5)

I am lowly and in pain; let your salvation, O God, protect me. (69:29)

I thank you that you have answered me and have become my salvation. (118:21)

Turn, O LORD, save my life; deliver me for the sake of your steadfast love. (6:4)

Save me from all my pursuers and deliver me. (7:1)

Be a rock of refuge for me, a strong fortress to save me. (31:2)

Save me, O God, by your name, and vindicate me by your might. (54:1)

Deliver me from those who work evil; from the bloodthirsty save me. (59:2)

Save all the oppressed of the earth. (76:9)

Save me from my persecutors, for they are too strong for me. (142:6)

They forgot God, their Savior, who had done great things in Egypt. (106:21)

All of these meanings of salvation in the Old Testament—as liberation from bondage, return from exile, and rescue from peril—continue in the New Testament, especially in the gospels and the letters of Paul. What they all have in common is salvation as "deliverance," "rescue." To be saved is to be delivered/rescued from that which ails us. Salvation is also about more than deliverance and rescue: to be saved is to enter into a new kind of life—a life covenanted with God, the central theme of both the Old and New Testaments. Salvation is about deliverance and transformation.

## More Images of Salvation

This root meaning of salvation and its siblings is also expressed in many biblical texts and images that do not explicitly use the word. For example, Isaiah 35 is filled with images of salvation as transformation, even though the word does not appear:

> The dry land shall be glad, the desert shall rejoice and blossom. . . . Waters shall break forth in the wilderness, and streams in the desert. (vv. 1, 6)

> Say to those who are of a fearful heart, "Be strong, do not fear! Here is your God." (v. 4)

> Then the eyes of the blind shall be opened, and the ears of the deaf unstopped; then the lame shall leap like a deer, and the tongue of the speechless sing for joy. (vv. 5–6)

The chapter concludes with the joy of salvation and the ending of sorrow:

> Everlasting joy shall be upon their heads; they shall obtain joy and gladness, and sorrow and sighing shall flee away. (v. 10)

Salvation as deliverance and transformation is expressed in a number of compact images found in both the Old and New Testaments. They occur so often that they are archetypal. I illustrate with texts from the New Testament.

*From Blindness to Seeing Again.* The Gospels contain stories of Jesus giving sight to blind people. Whatever the historical basis for these stories, it is clear that blindness and seeing have a metaphorical meaning as well. This is most apparent in John's Gospel where

Jesus is "the Light of the World" who opens the eyes of the blind and shines in the darkness. For John, "enlightenment"—seeing again, seeing truly—is a major image of salvation.

The metaphorical meaning of blindness and seeing is common to a number of sayings attributed to Jesus. They speak of sighted people who are nevertheless blind:

> There are those who have eyes but do not see. Just as, to switch to a hearing metaphor, there are those who have ears who do not hear. (Mark 8:18)

> There are blind guides (Matt. 23:16, 24)—obviously sighted people are being spoken of.

> If a blind person leads a blind person, they will both fall into a ditch (Matt. 15:14). Here also, sighted people are being spoken of.

*From Death to Life:* The Gospels contain stories of Jesus restoring people to life. Again, whatever the historical basis of these stories, their metaphorical meaning is clear. Just as there are sighted people who are blind, so also there are living people who are dead. Consider this provocative and brilliant one-liner from Jesus: "Let the dead bury their own dead" (Matt. 8:22). He obviously said this about living people. It is a serious indictment—we can be alive and yet dead. It also includes good news; there is a way of leaving the land of the dead.

The movement from death to life is also found in Paul's thinking. Paul speaks of dying and rising with Christ (e.g., Rom. 6:3–11) and of he himself having been "crucified with Christ" (Gal. 2:19) and entering into a new kind of life. In John's Gospel, this is the meaning of being "born again" (John 3:1–10).

*From Infirmity to Well-Being:* The Gospels contain many stories of Jesus healing people. At least some of these reflect historical reality—Jesus was known as a healer and exorcist. More stories are told about Jesus as healer than about any other figure in antiquity. But these stories also have a more-than-factual meaning. This is salvation as healing the wounds of existence, as well-being, as wholeness. Indeed, this is the etymology of the English word *salvation.* Its Latin roots are the same as those for the word *salve,* a healing ointment. Salvation is the healing of our wounds and becoming whole.

*From Fear to Trust:* The overcoming of fear and anxiety is a common concern in the Bible. "Fear not" and "Do not be afraid" are among its most frequent phrases. In a famous passage in the Gospels, Jesus counsels his followers not to worry, not to be anxious, but instead to trust in God (Luke 12:22–31). So also 1 Peter 5:7: "Cast all your anxiety upon him, because he cares for you."

## THE MORE-THAN-PERSONAL MEANINGS

Salvation concerns individuals; it is personal. But it is also consistently corporate in the Bible. It includes how we live together in communities, societies, and nations. In other words, salvation is about the kind of world we live in.

In the broad and important sense of the word, salvation in the Bible is "political" as well as personal. The word *politics* needs redeeming from its contemporary reduction to partisanship, nastiness, shadiness, and self-interest. The broad meaning of *politics* is ancient, reflected in its Greek root *polis,* which means "city." Politics concerns the shape and shaping of the city—by which is meant humans living together in large populations. Politics is thus about the shape and shaping of societies, nations, and the world itself. What should the humanly created world look like?

In this broad sense, salvation in the Bible is political, a dimension that is often missed when we are limited to understanding the word within the heaven-and-hell framework. A historical-metaphorical reading of scripture restores a crucial dimension to what the Bible means by salvation. Its political meaning is central to the story of the exodus, the prophets, Jesus, and Paul. The political meaning of salvation in the Bible has two focal points: justice and peace.

*From Injustice to Justice:* The primary justice issue in the Bible is economic justice. Many issues that we think of as justice issues today (like democracy, racism, human rights, gender equality, the environment) had not yet come up. For the most part, the Bible doesn't address them. Rather, its passion for justice is focused on economic justice.

There is an obvious reason for this—the world of the Bible was marked by massive economic injustice. The ruling elite acquired about two-thirds of the wealth in society, while around 90 percent of the population lived on the margin of subsistence and destitution. For the primary voices in the Bible, this is not what their God wanted. Rather, "The earth is the LORD's and all that is in it" (Ps. 24:1)—the earth belongs to God, not to us. We are but "aliens and tenants" on this earth (Lev. 25:23)—we do not own it. Yet we most often treat it as if we do own it—and some of us own more of it than others.

The economic justice that is the Bible's passion (and God's passion) concerns the basic necessities of life. In the Bible, they are land and food, the material basis of existence. Everybody should have enough, not as the product of charity, but as the result of the way the system is put together. The Bible knows that powerful and wealthy elites commonly structure the world in their own self-interest. Pharaoh and Herod and Caesar are still with us. From them we need to be saved.

*From Violence to Peace:* The second broad political meaning of salvation in the Bible is peace. Like many images of salvation, peace has both a personal and political meaning. The personal meaning is peace of mind and, slightly extended, peace with those with whom one is in intimate contact—family, neighbors, associates. But peace in the Bible is also about the end of violence and the cessation of war.

Along with economic injustice as institutionalized poverty and destitution, institutionalized violence was the other plague that caused the greatest amount of unnecessary human misery in the world of the Bible. There was the violence that the ruling elite used to keep the population in line. There was the violence of wars, which were most often started by the ruling elite against foreign elites for the sake of gaining their land and wealth. For the most part, ordinary people (90 percent of the population) had no stake in wars, even as they were often ruined by them by higher taxation; conscription; pillage of domestic animals; ruining of crops, resulting in famine; confiscation of land by an invader; and being slaughtered while fighting or as civilian victims of an invading army.

Thus it is not surprising that the second primary political meaning of salvation in the Bible is peace and nonviolence. Not just personal peace of mind and nonviolence in our personal relationships, but peace as the end of war. One of the best-known passages of the Old Testament occurs independently in two prophets, indicating how widespread this yearning was:

*Many peoples shall come and say,*
*"Come, let us go up to the mountain of the* LORD,
*to the house of the God of Jacob;*
*that he may teach us his ways*
*and that we may walk in his paths."*
*For out of Zion shall go forth instruction,*
*and the word of the* LORD *from Jerusalem.*
*He shall judge between the nations,*
*and shall arbitrate for many peoples;*
*they shall beat their swords in plowshares,*
*and their spears into pruning hooks;*
*nation shall not lift up sword against nation,*
*neither shall they learn war any more. (Isa. 2:3–4; Mic.*
    *4:2–3)*

So also in the Gospels. According to the Sermon on the Mount in Matthew, Jesus said, "Blessed are the peacemakers, for they will be called children of God (5:9) and "You have heard that it was said, 'You shall love your neighbor and hate your enemy.' But I say to you, Love your enemies" (5:43–44).

According to Luke, as Jesus wept over Jerusalem, which in his time had become the center of collaboration between the Temple authorities and Roman imperial officials, he said: "If you, even you, had only recognized on this day the things that make for peace!" (19:41–42). In Luke's story of Jesus's birth, the angel speaks of Jesus as a "Savior" and the heavenly chorus sings of Jesus as bringing peace on earth (2:11, 14). "Savior" as the one who brings peace on earth was one of the titles of the Roman emperor in the first century. But the emperor brought peace through military conquest. Imperial peace is the absence of resistance to imperial policy. The peace of which the Bible speaks is peace through justice.

Salvation as a world of justice and peace is the "dream of God" in the Bible, a phrase used by Verna Dozier, an African American author and theologian, and by retired South African archbishop Desmond Tutu.[7] God's dream, God's passion, is a transformed world of justice and peace.

An understanding of salvation that takes the Bible seriously will be both personal and political. It can inform us about personal transformation. Even some of the overtly political meanings of the exodus story have personal or psychological-spiritual meanings. Most of us as we grew up acquired a Pharaoh within who holds us in bondage, tells us to work harder, and gives us meager rations. This Pharaoh is most often the internalized voice of our socialization into a particular family in a particular culture, at a particular time and place, with its conventionally accepted demands. Many live for decades, sometimes for all of their lives, with a strong demanding critical voice within. Salvation is liberation from the Pharaoh within as well as from the Pharaoh without.

So also return from exile has a personal meaning. Some people are literally exiled to another country, where they live in conditions of disempowerment and impoverishment. But exile is also an archetypal image of the human condition. We often feel cut off, separated, exiled, alienated from life. Salvation as return from exile is return and reconnection to what matters, a center of meaning and purpose—to God. Our lives began in Eden, we were cast out of Eden, and we long to return. In words from St. Augustine, our hearts are restless until they find their home in God—until we return to and reconnect with, as Acts says, the one in whom we live and move and have our being.

So salvation is personal transformation. And it is also the transformation of this world, the humanly created world in which we live, into a better world. Salvation is a twofold transformation—of ourselves and the world.

I conclude with two stories. The first goes back forty years to graduate school. As one of my professors was lecturing on chapter 5 of Paul's letter to the Romans, he told a story about an Anglican priest confronted by an evangelical Christian.

"Are you saved?" the evangelical asked.

The priest responded, "It depends on what you mean by 'saved.' Do you mean 'Am I saved?' in the past, present, or future tense? If you mean 'Am I saved?' in the sense, 'Has God already done all that is necessary to save me?' then yes, certainly. If you mean 'Am I saved?' in the sense, 'Do I presently live in a saving relationship with God?' then my answer is yes, I trust. If you mean 'Am I saved?' in the sense, 'Have I already become all that I might become?' then certainly not."

Though the priest's response can be heard as rather haughty, it is also in accord with the Bible. There salvation does have three tenses. It is what God has done in the past. It is what can happen in the present. And it is also not yet—not completed, neither for us as individuals nor for the world.

The second story is from the last decade when I was speaking at a mainline clergy conference. I mentioned in my first lecture that whenever Christianity emphasizes the afterlife as the reason for being Christian, the result invariably is a distortion of Christianity. It becomes a religion of requirements and rewards; the message is "Be a Christian now for the sake of heaven later." It focuses our attention on the next life rather than on this world. It creates an in-group and an out-group; there are some who meet that criterion and some who don't. And so forth.

In the question-and-response period that followed, one of the clergy asked, "If Christianity's not about an afterlife, then what's our product?"

His question struck me as earnest, not confrontational or sarcastic. He was in his forties and thus had attended a mainline seminary not so long ago. I wondered how he could have done that without encountering a more biblical understanding of salvation. I realized that he didn't know what his message was if it wasn't about heaven.

I took his question seriously, for it's an important question. If Christianity is not primarily about an afterlife, if salvation is not primarily about an afterlife, then what is our "product"?

My answer, the answer pointed to by this chapter, is that our product is *salvation as the twofold transformation of ourselves and the world*. Moreover, I think most people yearn for this. We yearn for the transformation of our lives—for a fuller connection to what is, from liberation to all that keeps us in bondage, for sight, for wholeness, for the healing of the wounds of existence. And most of us yearn for a world that is a better place. We may have disagreements about how that is to be brought about. But most of us yearn for that—for ourselves and our contemporaries, for our children and grandchildren, and for the people and world of the future.

Salvation concerns these two transformations. It responds to our two deepest yearnings. Who does not want this? This is what Christianity at its best is about. And this is what the religions of the world at their best are about.

# CHAPTER 4

# The Bible

At a basic level, the referent of the word *Bible* is obvious—it names Christianity's holy book, its sacred scripture. Yet what it means to affirm this is not agreed upon. Indeed, conflict about the meaning of the Bible—its origin, authority, and interpretation—is the single most divisive issue in American Christianity today.

Before turning to the conflict, we begin with basic "facts" about the Bible, information about which there is no disagreement:

As Christian sacred scripture, it is foundational for Christianity.

The Christian Bible includes the Old and New Testaments. The first is the Christian name for the Jewish Bible. The second is the name of a collection of Christian documents from the century after Jesus. Though both are sacred scripture for Christians, the former is often relatively neglected.

All Christians agree that there are at least sixty-six books in the Bible: thirty-nine in the Old Testament and twenty-seven in the New Testament. Most Protestants restrict the Bible to these sixty-six. But for a majority of Christians—Catholic, Orthodox, and Anglican—there are more, an additional collection of books commonly called the Apocrypha, Jewish writings from the two centuries before Jesus. The most familiar are 1 and 2 Maccabees, Sirach (also known as Ecclesiasticus), Wisdom of Solomon, and Judith.

The Old Testament is almost four times as long as the New Testament. The Apocrypha is about four-fifths as long as the New Testament.

The Old Testament has three main parts: Torah, Prophets, and Writings. The Torah (also known as the Law or the Pentateuch) includes the first five books of the Bible, Genesis through Deuteronomy. The Prophets include not only prophets such as Isaiah, Jeremiah, Amos, and so forth, but also 1 and 2 Samuel and 1 and 2 Kings. The Writings include Psalms, Proverbs, Job, Ecclesiastes, and others.

The New Testament has four kinds of documents: four Gospels, Matthew, Mark, Luke, and John; twenty-one letters, attributed to figures such as Paul, Peter, James, and John; one narrative of early Christianity's spread from Jerusalem to Rome, Acts; and one anticipation of "the end," called Revelation by Protestants and the Apocalypse by Catholics.

To refer to biblical documents as *books* is common, but also somewhat misleading. In the modern world, *book* refers to a document of considerable length. But many biblical documents are not very long. A few are as brief as a page or two, many have fewer than a dozen pages, and most are under forty pages. The Greek root of the word *Bible* reflects this; it means "little books."

There is another difference. In our world, books are generally written for people whom the author doesn't know. But the writings included in the Bible were written for people whom the authors did know. The Old Testament was written from within and for the ancient Jewish people. The New Testament was written from within and for early Christian communities. So to the extent that *book* suggests a long document written for a reading public unknown to the author, it does not reflect the documents that make up the Bible.

None of the above statements is controversial. But beyond these basic facts, Christians disagree vigorously about the Bible's origin, authority, and interpretation.

The first way of seeing the Bible was briefly described in Chapter 2. For many Christians today, the Bible is the inerrant and infallible revelation of God, and it is to be interpreted literally and absolutely. To use a recently coined acronym, it is TAWOGFAT— "the authoritative Word of God for all time."[1]

Christian language about the Bible—that it is "inspired by God" and is "the Word of God"—reinforces this understanding. Moreover, the reading of a biblical text in worship services is often followed by the congregational response, "The Word of the Lord." Heard uncritically, as they often are, these words convey the notion that the Bible is the direct revelation of God.

This understanding of the Bible locates its absolute authority in its origin—it comes from God. It is "inspired by God" as no other book is. It has authority because of its divine origin. But millions of Christians have serious problems with this understanding of the word *Bible*. In the rest of this chapter, we describe an alternative understanding of the Bible's origin and authority.

## A HUMAN PRODUCT

The alternative understanding of the Bible's origin is grounded in the historical and theological scholarship of the last few centuries. That scholarship has made it clear that the Bible is a human product, not a divine one. The Old Testament is the product of ancient Israel, and the New Testament is the product of early Christian communities.

The historical evidence for this is overwhelmingly persuasive. Reading the Old Testament attentively, carefully, and historically makes it clear that this is the way voices within ancient Israel told its story. So also reading the New Testament attentively, carefully, and historically makes it clear that this is the way voices within early Christianity told the story of Jesus and his significance for the new life his followers had found in him.

To affirm this does not mean denying the reality of God or of God's inspiring presence in the lives of people in these ancient communities. But it does mean that the Bible tells Christians how our spiritual ancestors (the people of ancient Israel and early Christianity) saw things—and *not* how God sees things. The Bible includes their experiences of God, their stories about God, their understandings of life with God, and how we should live. But it is their story—*not* God's infallible, inerrant, and absolute story.

It includes their wisdom, insight, and convictions. It also includes their limitations, blind spots, and misapprehensions. Reading the Bible attentively, carefully, and historically makes this clear. Did God ever command that all the men, women, and children of our enemies be killed? Did God ever say that slavery was okay? Did God ever forbid remarriage after divorce? Did God ever command that adulterers be stoned? That children who dishonor their parents should be killed? That women should be silent in church? That same-sex relationships are an abomination? That God is violent? That Jesus is coming soon, and that his second coming will involve incredible suffering and death for most of humanity—indeed, the destruction of the world itself?

Or do passages in the Bible that teach these things (and more) tell us how some of our spiritual ancestors saw things? Do they not suggest—persuasively and overwhelmingly—that the Bible is their product, a human product, and not God's product?

## FORMATION OF THE CANON

But if the Bible's authority is not to be grounded in its origin in God, why then does it have authority for Christians? The answer is that our spiritual ancestors declared these documents to be authoritative, to be sacred scripture. They included them in the *canon* (from the Greek for "rule" or "standard") of the Bible.

Thus the sacred status of the books in the Bible is the product of a process, the formation of the canon. To explain, the books of the Bible were not seen as sacred scripture when they were written. For example, when Paul wrote letters to early Christian communities in the 50s of the first century, neither he nor his recipients considered them "sacred scripture" or imagined that they would someday become part of the Bible. Paul was simply writing letters to these communities in their particular circumstances. Only later were they declared to be sacred scripture, part of the Bible of a new religious movement.

The process of determining the books to be included in the canon occurred over many centuries. We do not have precise dates or records of official meetings at which decisions were made—

either because the records have been lost or because there never were official meetings about what to include in the Bible. To report the common scholarly estimates of the process whereby the books of the Old Testament came to be included in the canon:

The first part to become sacred was the Law, the five books that make up the Torah (or Pentateuch). These books begin with creation and end with the ancient Israelites on the border of the promised land. Most of their narration is set in the 1200s BCE. They were canonized—that is declared to be sacred scripture—by about 400 BCE.

The second part to become sacred was the Prophets. As mentioned early in this chapter, these include historical books such as Joshua and Judges, Samuel and Kings as well as collected sayings of the people we think of as the prophets of ancient Israel. They cover a period of time from around 1200 to 400 BCE. They were considered part of the canon by about 200 BCE.

The third section of the Jewish Bible to become sacred was the Writings, which include Psalms, Proverbs, Job, Ecclesiastes, Esther, and others. They were canonized by about 100 CE.

Until recently, scholars have commonly said that the finalization of the canon of the Jewish Bible occurred at an official Jewish gathering known as the Council of Jamnia (or Yavneh) around 90 CE. Confidence about this is no longer widespread. But that the Writings were the last part of the Old Testament to be canonized and that this happened around 100 CE are widely accepted by mainstream scholars. This conclusion is supported by the way the

New Testament refers to the Bible as "the law and the prophets" and not as "the law, the prophets, and the writings."

So also the canon of the New Testament is the result of a process that took centuries. As in the case of the Old Testament, we have no record of any councils officially deciding what should be included in it, even though some recent authors say that it happened at the Council of Nicea in 325 CE. It didn't.

We do know that even after 325, there was not yet common agreement about the extent of the New Testament. Eusebius, a Christian bishop and historian writing around 330, said that there were twenty-one books about which there was common agreement. Those not yet universally agreed upon were James, Jude, 2 Peter, 2 and 3 John, and Revelation.

The first list of the twenty-seven books that we know as the New Testament comes from 367 CE in a letter from Bishop Athanasius. We do not know what happened between the time of Eusebius and Athanasius or whether what Athanasius wrote was common Christian conviction by 367. Even after Athanasius, some Christian lists of the New Testament canon do not include exactly the same twenty-seven. The book of Revelation was the last to be universally recognized. In parts of the Eastern church, it was not included until the 700s, maybe even later.

The important point is that the Bible is sacred scripture not because of its origin, but because our ancestors in the faith declared these particular books to be sacred, that is, authoritative. That is why the Bible has authority—not because it was uniquely and directly inspired by God.

To suggest an analogy, the Constitution of the United States has authority for Americans not because of its origin, but because our national ancestors ratified it—that is, declared it to be authoritative. To be an American is to live within a community that accepts the Constitution as the authority and foundation for life together.

The analogy is imperfect. The Constitution is a legal document, and even though the Bible contains laws and ethical teachings, it is much more than a legal document. It is filled with stories, letters, praise, prayers, and so forth. To interpret the Bible as if it were a legal document is a mistake.

But the analogy does work for our purposes. The Bible has authority for Christians for the same reason that the Constitution has authority for Americans. To be Christian means to live within a community that accepts the Bible as its authoritative scripture. To be Christian involves a continuing conversation with the Bible as the foundation of Christianity. If that dialogue were to cease, we would cease to be Christians. The Bible is constitutive of Christian life and identity.

This way of seeing the Bible's origin and authority goes with the historical-metaphorical interpretation of the Bible described in Chapter 2. We best understand the Bible when we set its texts in their ancient contexts and when we are attentive to their metaphorical meanings as well—that is, their more-than-literal, more-than-factual, more-than-historical meanings.

## THE BIBLE AS THE "WORD OF GOD"

We conclude with a familiar phrase, the Bible as the "Word of God," the "Word of the Lord." What does it mean to say this? Some Christians, especially Protestants, think that it means that what the Bible says comes from God—as if it means that the Bible is the "*words* of God." *Word* (singular and capitalized) has become *words* (lowercase and plural).

But throughout its long history, Christianity has called the Bible the "Word of God," not the "words of God," thereby signaling that *Word* is being used in a special and metaphorical sense. Think of the metaphorical meaning of *word,* of *language.* It is a means of communication, of disclosure, of bridging the gap between two parties. To speak of the Bible as the "Word of God" means that it is a vehicle, a means, of communing with God. It is sacramental—divine not in its origin or authority, but in its purpose and function in the Christian life. It is a means whereby the Spirit of God continues to speak to us.

Confirmation and illumination of this way of understanding the "Word of God" is provided by another familiar Christian use of the phrase, namely, Jesus as the "Word of God." In John's Gospel, he is the "Word" become flesh, the "Word" embodied in a human life, the "Word" incarnate. Obviously, Jesus was not literally a word, a sound, letters on a page, or a collection of words. He was a person. A book can be the "Word of God." A person can be the "Word of God."

For Christians, the "Word of God" as known, revealed, disclosed, and embodied in Jesus is the decisive "Word of God." It outranks the Bible. Jesus is the norm of the Bible. When the Bible and what we see in Jesus conflict, as they sometimes do, Jesus trumps the Bible. This is what it means to say that Jesus is the Word become flesh. In him, Christians see more clearly than anywhere else the character and passion of God.

So, is the Bible the "Word of God," a means of revelation? Yes. Does it matter? Yes. Does it matter as much as the "Word" become flesh, the "Word" we see embodied in Jesus? No. Of course, we wouldn't know about Jesus without the Bible. To echo language from Paul, we have this treasure in earthen vessels. The Bible is an earthen vessel that contains our treasure. To echo language from Martin Luther, the Bible is the manger in which we find Christ.

# CHAPTER 5

# God

The word *God* is utterly central to Christianity. In this chapter, we focus on the *referent* of *God* and synonyms like *the Spirit* and *the Sacred*. What do we think of when we hear or use these words? Both those who affirm and those who deny the reality of God have something in mind when they do so.

Two very different understandings of the referent of the word *God* are found in the Christian tradition, beginning in the Bible and coexisting in Christianity ever since.[1] For the first, *God* refers to a being beyond the universe, another being in addition to the universe. Of course, the word refers to a very special kind of being, the supreme being, almighty and all-knowing. A long time ago, this being created the universe, and God and the universe are related to each other as artist to art, furniture maker to furniture, designer to product. They are separate from each other, even as the latter is the product of the former.

For the second, the word *God* does not refer to a being separate from the universe, but to a sacred presence all around us—a reality that is more than the space-time world of matter and energy, even as it also present everywhere and permeates everything in the space-time world. God is not a being "somewhere else" (up there,

or out there, or beyond), but "right here" as well as "more than
right here."[2]

## GOD AS A BEING

To explore these two referents in greater detail, the first referent
is the most common meaning in modern English. It shapes the
understanding of many Christians as well as agnostics and atheists. Consider the following dictionary definitions of *God* (italics
added):

> *Oxford American:* "Without an article: In Christianity and
> other monotheistic religions the creator and ruler of the
> universe and source of all moral authority; *the supreme being*."

> *Random House Webster's:* "The creator and ruler of the universe;
> *Supreme Being.* One of several immortal powers, esp. one with
> male attributes, presiding over some portion of worldly affairs."

> *American Heritage:* "*A perfect being* conceived as the creator
> of the universe, and worshiped in monotheistic religions; the
> force, effect, or a manifestation or aspect of this being; *a being*
> of supernatural powers or attributes, believed in and worshiped
> by a people, esp. a male deity."

Note that according to all three definitions God is *a being,* separate and distinct from the universe—just as all the beings we know
are distinct and separate from each other. Perhaps the most familiar and concise biblical expression of this understanding is found in
the opening words of the Lord's Prayer: "Our Father in heaven."
God is a personlike being who is not here, but "in heaven."

*A Personlike Being:* People who think of God this way commonly think that the word refers not only to a being, but one with personal characteristics. God is like a person—a center of consciousness who thinks, knows, wills, feels, acts, loves, cares, and, commonly, judges and punishes.

*An Authority Figure:* This personlike being is an authority figure. As the dictionary definitions put it, the word *God* refers to the "ruler of the universe" and the "source of all moral authority." God has revealed what is right and wrong—what we are to believe and how we are to live. Moreover, as an authority figure, God will judge us. God is like a strict parent, even though also like a loving parent. How to reconcile these two—God as strict and loving parent—continues to be puzzled over by those who think of God as the ultimate authority figure, who not only reveals, but also enforces God's requirements.

*An Interventionist:* God as a personlike being relates to the universe through intervention—the only way a being separate from the universe can act within it. Many passages in the Bible presuppose this, for example, stories of spectacular events caused directly by God and prayers petitioning God to cause a certain outcome. Many Christians today believe in divine intervention, even though some would say that it happens now in less spectacular ways than in biblical times.

*As Male:* It has been common for centuries to use male language for God. Consider how frequently God is referred to as "Father," "King," and "Lord" and how male pronouns are commonly used for God. Two of the dictionary definitions explicitly mention that *God* refers to a "male" deity. Although an increasing number of mainline Christians now use gender-inclusive language for God, many still speak and think of God as "he." Some vigorously resist any change in male language for God, especially more conservative Christians.

*As Real:* This is the God about whose existence one can argue. The existence or nonexistence of God is the presupposition of "proofs" for God's existence. All begin with the supposition that there may or may not be such a being and then advance arguments that are meant to convince. Whatever the rational value of the proofs, "believers" are those who believe that there is such a being. Nonbelievers are those who do not. The argument, the difference between the affirmation and the negation, is the answer to the question: Is there, in addition to the universe, a superpowerful personlike being?

Not only do many Christians understand the word *God* this way, but most agnostics and atheists also do. When someone says to me, "I don't believe in God," I always respond, "Tell me about the God you don't believe in." Invariably, this is their understanding of God. The authors of recent bestsellers on atheism also understand the word in this way; it is the existence of this referent of the word *God* that they reject. They show little or no awareness that there is another way of thinking about what this word points to.

## GOD AS SACRED PRESENCE

The other referent of the word *God* is very different. The word does not refer to a being separate from the universe, but to an encompassing sacred reality all around us and within us. As ancient as the first, it is a basic view in Judaism, Christianity, and Islam from antiquity to the present; it is also affirmed in other major religions and in many smaller indigenous religions around the world.

In the Bible, the most concise expression of this referent of the word is in the book of Acts. In language attributed to Paul, God is "the one in whom we live and move and have our being" (17:28). Note how the language works. Where are we in relation to God? We are *in* God. We *live within* God. We *move within* God. We *have our being within* God. God is not a being far off, "out there," somewhere beyond the universe, separate from us and the world. Rather, the word refers to "the one" in whom everything that is, is—a reality that encompasses us and all that is.

Psalm 139 provides a more extended biblical example. The author addresses God and asks, "Where can I go from your spirit? Or where can I flee from your presence?" (v. 7). Then the psalmist affirms God's presence everywhere:

> *If I ascend to heaven, you are there;*
> *if I make my bed in Sheol [the depths of the earth], you*
> *   are there.*
> *If I . . . settle at the farthest limits of the sea,*
> *even there your hand shall lead me,*
> *and your right hand shall hold me fast. (vv. 8–10)*

The text refers to the three-story universe of the ancient imagination: heaven above, Sheol beneath, and earth—"the farthest limits of the sea"—in between. No matter where the psalmist imagines going, God is there, present. How can this be? Only if the word *God* is understood to refer to a sacred presence who is everywhere. That is why there is nowhere one can be and be outside God.

To use a simple analogy, we are in God as fish are in water. The water is all around; fish move within the water, live within the water, have their being within the water. The water is not separate from the fish—and yet the water is more than the fish. So also God is not a being separate from the universe, but a reality that is more than the universe—even as God includes the universe.

This understanding continues in the postbiblical Christian tradition. Irenaeus, an early Christian theologian around 200, wrote: "God contains everything and is contained by nothing." Again, note how the language works: everything is in God ("God contains everything"), and yet God is more than everything ("contained by nothing"). It is affirmed by major theologians throughout the history of Christianity: in the premodern world by Augustine, Thomas Aquinas, and others, including especially the great Christian mystics, and in the modern period by the Protestant Paul Tillich and the Catholic Karl Rahner, two of the most important theologians of the twentieth century.

The notion that God is not a being separate from the universe but a sacred presence all around us strikes some Christians as unfamiliar, even strange. But it should not. Those of us who grew up in churches not only heard God referred to as "Our Father in heaven." We also heard that God is "everywhere"—that is, omnipresent. How can that be? It is possible only if the word does not refer to "a being," a "superbeing," or a "personal being" separate from the universe, but to the reality in whom we and everything exist.

This referent of the word radically changes the question of God's existence. It is no longer about whether there is another being separate from the universe. Rather, the question is about the nature of reality, of "what is," of "is-ness." "What is," "reality," or "is-ness" is—does anybody want to debate that? The question is not *whether* "is-ness" is, but *what* "is-ness" is. Is "what is" simply the space-time world of matter and energy? Or is reality—"is-ness"—"more" than that?

This referent of the word *God* affirms that reality, "what is," is ultimately a sacred reality, a "more," all around us, wondrous and glorious. The word does not point to a being who may or may not exist, but names "what is" as wondrous and sacred, a stupendous and glorious "more."[3] Importantly, this understanding of the word does not simply identify *God* with the space-time universe of matter and energy. *God* is not simply poetic language for the universe as we have come to know it. Rather, the space-time universe of matter and energy is "in God." "The more" is all around us, but not simply to be identified with the totality of what can be known through ordinary and scientific means.

This understanding of the referent of *God* changes many things. It changes how we think of God as creator. The first understanding of the word *God* goes with thinking of creation as an event in the past, whether six thousand or fifteen billion years ago, when God created the universe as something separate from God's self. For the second understanding, to affirm God as creator means that the universe in every moment of time is dependent upon God for its existence. The universe is in God, moves within God, has its existence within God. If God ceased creating the world, everything would vanish. Creation is about the universe's dependence upon God, not primarily about its origin in the past.

It changes how we think of God's relationship to the world. Intervention disappears, because the notion of intervention presupposes that God is a being separate from the universe and thus normally "not here," so God acts within the world only through occasional interventions. But if *God* refers to a reality that is "right here" and "all around us," then the language of intervention is not necessary. Indeed, it doesn't work.

God's involvement in the world does not disappear. Rather than speaking about divine intervention, this way of thinking about God speaks about *divine presence, intention,* and *interaction.* Divine presence: God is not absent but everywhere present. Divine intention: according to the Bible, God, the sacred, has a purpose. Divine interaction: our relationship to the sacred, our openness to the sacred, our participation in the sacred, makes possible things that otherwise might not be possible. There can be cooperation—interaction—between divine purpose and human action. All of the above are affirmed, even as the notion of intervention is set aside.

This understanding of the referent of the word *God* is orthodox Christian theology—more orthodox than thinking of God as a separate being. To use semitechnical theological terms, the foundational voices of the Bible and the Christian tradition have affirmed that the reality to which *God* refers is both *transcendent* and *immanent.* To say that God is transcendent means that God is more than the universe. To say that God is immanent means that God is everywhere.

To think that the word *God* refers to a personlike being separate from the universe speaks only of God's transcendence. In shorthand, this is commonly called *supernatural theism:* God is a supernatural being separate from the universe.

To affirm both—that God is transcendent, more than the universe, even as God is also immanent, a presence pervading the universe—is the ancient biblical and Christian referent of the word *God.* To use a modern term coined in the early 1800s, this way of thinking about God is called *panentheism*. The Greek roots of the word mean "everything is in God." This is the orthodox and authentic meaning of the word.

## PERSONIFYING GOD

We return to the fact that the Bible and postbiblical Christian language often speak of God as a personlike being, as in the Lord's Prayer. God is personified not only as a father, but also as a king, shepherd, judge, lover, mother, and so forth. Does realizing that *God* does not refer to a separate person mean personification should be avoided? No. There is nothing wrong with personifying God. It is the natural language of worship, devotion, and relationship. Problems occur only when personifications of God are understood literally or semiliterally. When this happens, the result is supernatural theism, with the limitations inherent in that view.

Avoiding the language of personification can easily create the impression that the word *God* refers to an "it"—a reality less than personal, an inanimate reality—and the etymology of *inanimate* means "un-spirited," without Spirit. But another option is seeing *God* as referring to a reality that is more than personal, not less than personal. This reality is sometimes known, experienced, as a *presence*—as having more the quality of a "you" than the quality of an "it." Thus personal language for God is appropriate, so long as "the one in whom we live and move and have our being" is not reduced to "a person," a supernatural person about whose existence one can argue. Reality, "is-ness," "what is" is. The question is not whether "is-ness" exists, but what it is like. Personal language affirms that this reality is more than personal, not less than personal.

# BEYOND ALL WORDS

One more very important point remains. The reality to which the word *God* points is beyond all words, beyond all language, beyond all concepts. In language attributed to Lao Tzu in sixth-century BCE China, "The Tao [the sacred] that can be named is not the eternal Tao." Once we name it, we are no longer talking about it, for this reality cannot be expressed in words.

This understanding is deeply embedded in Judaism and Christianity. As Moses experiences the sacred in the bush that burned without being consumed, he asks, "What is your name?" The answer is, "I AM WHO I AM." The sentence is a tautology; the second half says the same as the first half, and thus says nothing at all—except that God "is" and is beyond all names. The Jewish prohibition of images of God makes the same point, as does the prohibition against saying the most sacred name of God. So also do the voices of Jewish and Christian mystics when they say that the one, the sacred, is ineffable—beyond all language.

Thus humility and reticence in our language about God is called for. No concept of God, no way of stating the referent of the word—neither supernatural theism nor panentheism—is adequate. Yet the latter is better. More expansive and less constricting, it avoids the limitations that have made supernatural theism problematic or impossible for many.

# CHAPTER 6

# God's Character

How we think of God includes a second crucial element. In the Bible, the word God refers not only to a glorious and radiant "more," but to a "more" with "character." By "character," I mean what we mean when we speak about the "character" of individuals. What are they like at a deep level—a level that shapes all that they say and do? So also God's "character" means "what God is like."

When you hear or think the word *God,* whether you believe in God or not, what do you imagine God's character to be like? For example, do you think of an indifferent reality? A threatening, stern, punitive reality? A gracious, loving, compassionate reality? Some combination of those traits? Or something totally different?

In nonreligious language, the question being asked here is, "What is reality like?" Whether you believe in God or not or are uncertain, what do you think "is-ness" is like? Our answer matters greatly. Whether consciously aware of it or not, our sense of "what reality is like" shapes how we live.

The premise of this chapter is that there are three primary ways of thinking about the "character" of God—in nonreligious language, the "character" of reality.[1] The first sees God as indifferent, the second as threatening and dangerous, the third as gracious and life-giving.

## GOD AS INDIFFERENT

The first paradigm sees the character of God as indifferent and basically uninvolved with us in any purposive way. Reality—"is-ness"—simply is. "What is" is indifferent to human needs and ends. This is a common modern vision of reality. The universe is constituted by impersonal forces and energies. It has no character or purpose. Or if it does, it is a movement toward greater complexity of life.

Some who see "what is" in this way can be deeply appreciative of the wonder and glory of reality. But no matter how wondrous and glorious, reality simply "is." It has no "character"—or, perhaps more accurately, the character of "what is" is indifferent to us and all that we value.

Though this understanding is mostly modern, it was occasionally found in antiquity. Some voices from the distant past saw reality this way—typically voices of lament speaking from great suffering. God or the gods were indifferent. But it was not the common view, even as some sometimes wondered if it was "the way things are."

In the seventeenth and eighteenth centuries, this view began to appear among some Christian thinkers. Known as *Deists* and sometimes as *rationalists,* they sought to accommodate Christianity to the intellectual dynamic of the Enlightenment. Though they continued to affirm the reality of God, they saw the universe as operating within the framework of discoverable regularities, commonly thought of as natural laws. God was the creator of the universe "back then," "in the beginning," including its natural laws. Since then, God has not needed to do anything. Implicitly or explicitly, God has not been involved since "the beginning."

Few Christians today would identify themselves as Deists. Many do not know the word. But this understanding is present in contemporary Christianity. Some reconcile God as creator with the understanding of the universe as operating in accord with natural laws in the same way that the Deists did; God set it up in the beginning as something separate from God, and since then it has run on its own. God is a distant creator—not here, not present, not involved in the process. It is often accompanied by what has been called *practical atheism,* a way of living and being that assumes that God is not involved in the process of the universe and our lives.

For the majority of Christians, the second and third ways of seeing the character of God are more common. In radical shorthand, the first sees God's character as punitive and threatening; the second sees God's character as gracious and life-giving. Each understanding leads to a very different vision of the Christian life. Often they are combined, but it is an uneasy combination. Ultimately, they are polar opposites. They produce two very different forms of Christianity.

## GOD AS PUNITIVE AND THREATENING

We begin with an irony. Though Christian language regularly speaks of God as loving, many Christians see God's character very differently. God is seen as the source and enforcer of requirements, whether of belief or behavior or both. God—or at least the wrath of God—is much to be feared. Even though God loves us, God is also punitive.

So it was for me as I was growing up. We sang "Jesus Loves Me"; we heard "God is love"; and the first Bible verse I memorized began, "For God so loved the world." Yet I also heard that God was a lawgiver and judge—like a strict parent or righteous king who punishes when it is called for, whether in this life or after death.

The punitive image of God's character is a core element of the heaven-and-hell framework for understanding Christian language described in Chapter 1. It has haunted the lives of Christians for centuries. Imagine how the threat of hell operated in the minds of our ancestors during all of the centuries in which heaven and hell were taken for granted as postmortem possibilities. Many must have wondered if they were adequately right with God or if they faced the fires of hell. Some Christians still do. The message of many Christian churches, explicitly or implicitly, is that we need to measure up to the requirements of the punitive God. Where will you spend eternity?

There is, however, an escape from the punishment that we all deserve. We can be saved from the consuming fire that will devour much of humankind. God makes exceptions, and the basis for an exception is believing that Jesus appeased God's wrath by dying in our place. Those who believe in him will be spared.

But even the possibility of escape does not change the image of God's character as punitive; God has requirements and will enforce them. God is the rejected lawgiver, disappointed parent, angry king, jilted lover, who will punish those who don't "get it right."

Seeing reality as threatening and fearful also has nonreligious forms. Its psychotic form is paranoia—the conviction that reality is pervasively dangerous. The notion that life is full of threats also has a much more common form, a fear-based orientation to life. We are afraid about our physical security—our appearance, safety, and health. We are afraid about our financial security—about whether we have or will have enough. We are afraid about our national security, anxious to defend ourselves and our way of life against those we see as threatening—whatever it takes.

Think of how often advertising appeals to these fears. Think of how often political campaigns invoke these fears. Seeing reality as dangerous leads to a self-protective orientation toward life—What must I do, what must we do, to protect ourselves? Many of us live in a state of collective and consensual paranoia—fearing what our culture has taught us to fear and, for some of us, what our religion has taught us to fear.[2] Fear-based religion, fear-based individual behavior, and fear-based politics most often go together.

The punitive and threatening image of God's character is found in both Testaments. The common Christian stereotype of the God of the Old Testament (and Judaism) as wrathful, punitive, and judgmental and the God of the New Testament (and Christianity) as gracious, loving, and forgiving is simply wrong. Rather, texts and voices in both the Old and New Testaments speak of a punitive God. No wonder it has shaped much of Christianity in the centuries since.

Within this framework, how shall we live? What is the Christian life about? If God is a threatening and punitive judge, then life with God is about measuring up to whatever God requires of us in order to avoid God's punishment. The life of requirements and rewards, it is fearful of failure. But both Testaments also contain texts and voices that speak of God's character very differently. They lead to a very different image of what life with God is like, what the Christian life is about.

## GOD AS GRACIOUS, LOVING, AND COMPASSIONATE

The third possibility of seeing the character of God—of what reality, "is-ness," is like—is very different from the first two. Rather than referring to an indifferent or threatening and punitive reality, *God* refers to a gracious, loving, and compassionate reality. God—"what is"—is life-giving and life-affirming, willing our transformation and the transformation of the world and involved in those transformations.

The words *gracious, loving,* and *compassionate* are virtual synonyms and are frequent in both Testaments. *Gracious* and its sibling *grace* emphasize that life, our life, is a gift. We did not create ourselves. None of us is self-made. All that we are and whatever we have are gifts.

*Loving* and *compassionate* mean that God wills our well-being and the well-being of all creation. As the opening words of John 3:16 proclaim, God loves the world. In the story of creation in the first chapter of Genesis, after each day of creation God affirms the goodness of what has been created and at the end of the sixth day pronounces it all "very good." God's compassion, which we will explore more fully in Chapter 11, is also a central theme in both the Old and New Testaments.

Seeing God's character as gracious, loving, and compassionate emphasizes that our lives with God are not about measuring up to God's requirements for salvation. Rather, life with God is about a deepening relationship with God, not about satisfying requirements of belief and behavior. God has been in relationship with us from our beginning, whether we know that, believe that, or not.

Within this framework, in the Christian life, the religious life, we enter into a conscious and intentional relationship with God.

It is conscious—we become aware of our relationship with God. It is intentional—we will a deepening relationship with this reality. God is not to be feared and appeased, but to be embraced and loved.

This third way of seeing God's character makes a very different kind of life possible. Life is no longer fear-based. We do not need to protect the self from threats—whether from God or the world. Rather, we learn to center more deeply in God and trust more deeply in God.

It leads to a life free from fear, whatever happens. To see God's character as gracious, loving, and compassionate does not mean that bad things do not happen. God does not intervene to prevent these. But in the midst of the vagaries of life, the Bible proclaims again and again, in what may be its most frequent phrases, "Fear not," "Do not be afraid," "Do not worry." The Christian life is about trusting ever more deeply in God—"even when steeples are falling," to use words from a hymn written in the 1600s during the destruction and desolation of the Thirty Years' War.

## THE PASSION OF GOD

The *passion* and *character* of God are intrinsically related. By the *passion* of God, I mean what we mean when we ask of somebody, "What's your passion in life—what do you care most about, what are you passionate about?" Passion flows out of character.

So, what is God passionate about? When I was a child and an adolescent, what was most obvious was that God was passionate about personal behavior. This meant obeying the Ten Commandments. I cannot remember how old I was when I had memorized them. Six? Eight? Obeying them was not only about outward observance, but also about internal purity. No murder—but also no anger. No adultery (not an issue for a child or young teen)—but also no lustful thoughts. What God was passionate about was obedience, external and internal. Does personal behavior matter? Certainly. But God's passion as disclosed in the Bible is about much more.

Recall the meanings of salvation described in Chapter 3. All of them are about God's passion. God's passion is that we be liberated from bondage in Egypt, that we return from exile in Babylon, that we live together in a world of justice and peace, that we be delivered from peril, that our eyes be opened, that we become healed and whole, that we leave an old life behind and enter into a new life, that we be freed from anxiety and fear, and so forth. God's passion is our well-being and the well-being of all of creation.

Although many people see God as either indifferent, punitive, or gracious, others try to combine some of these attributes. The most popular option is trying to combine the gracious God with the punitive God. Consider how John 3:16 is sometimes understood. Its opening words affirm the gracious loving God: "For God so loved the world." I know of no Christians who disagree. Yet some Christians affirm, in effect, that God so loved the world that God sent Jesus to save us—and whoever doesn't believe in him will burn in hell forever.

Attempts to combine the gracious God with the punitive God invariably lead to conditional grace. There is an *if,* a condition. God loves us and will save us *if . . .* The content of the condition varies: if we believe in Jesus, if we believe that the Bible is the inerrant revelation of God, if we earnestly repent, if we behave in accord with God's will, if we are reasonably decent people. But whenever God's grace and love are made conditional, the punitive God triumphs.

The history of Christianity has been filled with the conflict between these two understandings of the character and passion of God. Is God gracious, loving, and compassionate? Or punitive and violent? Is God's passion the well-being of the whole of creation? Or the punishment of evildoers? The conflict is both personal and political. On the personal level, does God threaten us with violence for our wrongdoing? On the political level, does God will violence against our enemies?

So what is the character and passion of your God? The answer, for Christians, is what we see in Jesus. He is, as we emphasize in the next chapter, the decisive revelation of God's character and passion.

# CHAPTER 7

# Jesus

The central claim of Christianity is that Jesus is the decisive revelation of God. He reveals, discloses, what can be seen of God in a human life. This is the cumulative meaning of familiar Christian language about him: "Son of God," "Messiah," "Lord," the "Light of the World," "the Way, the Truth, and the Life." He is the "Word of God" become flesh, embodied, incarnated in a human life. He is the revelation, the epiphany of what God is like—of God's character and passion.

Seeing the decisive revelation of God in *a person* distinguishes Christianity from other religions. To use its two closest relatives as examples, Jews find the decisive revelation of God in a book, the Torah. Moses is the revealer, but not the revelation. Muslims find the decisive revelation of God in a book, the Qur'an. Muhammad is the revealer, but not the revelation. But for Christians, the decisive revelation of God is *a person,* not a sacred book. This distinction is not about superiority, but about difference.

Yet despite Jesus's importance for Christianity, his name is problematic for many in our time. For some, it has negative associations because it has been part of a fear-based Christianity that emphasized our sinfulness, guilt, unworthiness, and the threat of hell. Precisely because we have been so bad, Jesus had to die for us. More than one Christian has said to me, "I'm still struggling with Jesus. He has so much baggage."

For others, the issue is puzzlement about Christian language about Jesus. He is both human and divine. What does that mean? He was born of a virgin. Literally? Or if not, what does that mean? Able to perform miracles that no human could. If so, was he then really one of us? Died in our place for our sins. If so, does that mean that God required his death—that it was God's will? Raised from the dead. Literally? And if not, what does that mean?

## Pre-Easter and Post-Easter

Reclaiming and redeeming the word *Jesus* begins with the realization that it has two quite different even though related referents: the pre-Easter Jesus and the post-Easter Jesus. The first—also called the "historical Jesus"—refers to what he was like before his death. The second—sometimes called the "Christ of faith," though I do not use that expression myself—refers to what he became after his death. Both are to be affirmed, although it is important to see how they differ significantly from each other.

The pre-Easter Jesus refers to Jesus as a historical figure of the past, a Galilean Jew, born around 4 BCE and crucified around 30 CE. A flesh-and-blood human being like us, he was a particular height and weight, had to eat and drink, and was mortal. He had a beginning and an ending.

This Jesus doesn't exist anymore. He is dead and gone. To say this does not deny Easter. But it recognizes that what Easter means is not that a flesh-and-blood, corpuscular, protoplasmic Jesus still lives somewhere, is still a particular height and weight and still needs to eat and drink. Easter and the resurrection are not about the restoration of Jesus to his previous state. The post-Easter Jesus refers to what Jesus became after his death in Christian experience, reflection, and tradition.

What we call Easter is grounded in the experience of his early followers. We will explore the meaning of Easter more fully in Chapter 9. For now, I emphasize that that some of his followers experienced Jesus after his death—but in a radically new way. They had experienced the pre-Easter Jesus as a human being, indeed an extraordinarily remarkable human being, but nevertheless as somebody who was in one place at a time, who ate and slept, who was a particular size, and who could be arrested and killed.

After his death, they experienced him very differently. For example, Paul experienced him in a vision on his way to Damascus. Others had visions as well—Paul even provides a list (1 Cor. 15:5–8). So also the Gospels report visual experiences (e.g., Luke 24:13–35; John 20:24–29). Some Christians take these quite literally as meaning that the flesh-and-blood Jesus was raised from the dead. But it is nevertheless clear that the post-Easter Jesus is no longer a corporeal figure constrained by time and space; he can appear anywhere, pass through walls, be unrecognized, and suddenly vanish. Experiences like these led to conviction that Jesus is not simply a figure of the past, dead and gone, but a living reality of the present. This is the first meaning of Easter.

Experiences of the post-Easter Jesus led to a second conviction. Jesus is not only still with us, but is a divine reality. The new way in which his followers experienced him after his death led to the exclamation, "My Lord and my God." The words are from the disciple Thomas in John 20:28. Paul's experience of Jesus as a figure of the present led to his most characteristic shorthand summary of who Jesus is: "Jesus is Lord."

As one more example, in the final words of Matthew's Gospel, the risen Jesus promises his abiding presence with his followers: "And remember, I am with you always, to the end of the age" (28:20). The words echo the meaning of the name Emmanuel— "God-with-us" (see 1:23). Like God, the post-Easter Jesus is an abiding presence—omnipresent. This makes sense only if the post-Easter Jesus is one with God—indeed, divine like God.

The term *post-Easter Jesus* also refers to how Jesus is spoken of in the traditions that developed among his followers after his historical lifetime. Early Christian tradition about Jesus includes the whole of the New Testament, including the four Gospels. Written in the last third of the first century, they express how the traditions about Jesus had developed in their respective communities by that time. The earliest, Mark, was written around 70, about forty years after the death of Jesus. John is probably the latest, most likely written in the 90s.

As the products of developing traditions, the Gospels combine *memory* and *testimony*. Some of what they narrate is early Christian memory of things Jesus said and did. Read discerningly, they provide glimpses of the pre-Easter Jesus. They also contain testimony, the significance that Jesus had acquired in the experience and thought of his followers in the decades between Easter and the writing of the Gospels.

The rest of the New Testament is also the product of developing traditions. The seven genuine letters of Paul are the earliest; written in the 50s, they are thus earlier than the Gospels. They tell us how Paul saw Jesus and his significance some two to three decades after his historical life. The latest writings in the New Testament are from the early to the mid-second century. All reflect the way tradition had developed by the time they were written.

In these developing traditions, Jesus is given *titles,* the word given to the exalted language his followers used for him, words and phrases like "Messiah," "Son of God," "Lord," "Savior of the world," "Word of God," "Light of the World," "Bread of Life," "Great High Priest," and so forth. There is a near unanimous consensus among mainstream biblical scholars that these titles are post-Easter and do not go back to Jesus himself. He didn't talk about himself this way. Instead, these titles are the testimony of his followers to who he had become for them—in their experience, life, and thought. They—like the Nicene Creed of the 300s, which speaks of Jesus as "very God of very God" and "of one substance with the Father"—belong to the post-Easter Jesus of Christian tradition.

The distinction between the pre-Easter Jesus and the post-Easter Jesus matters greatly. Not because God requires us to get our beliefs right—correct beliefs have often been overvalued by Christians. Rather, it matters for us. To put it negatively, failing to see the distinction creates confusion. To put it positively, seeing the distinction is greatly illuminating.

When we do not make the distinction, the result is a hybrid Jesus. Everything that is said about the post-Easter Jesus is projected back onto the pre-Easter Jesus. The result is that even as a human being, he was divine—"very God of very God," "of one substance" with God. Even as a human being, he was the "second person" of the Trinity. Even as a human being, he had divine powers—and that's why he could walk on water, feed a multitude with a few loaves and fishes, change water into wine, and raise Lazarus from the dead. Even as human being, he had the mind of God, and that's why he could speak with authority and why we should take him seriously.

But all of this makes the pre-Easter Jesus more than human—and thus not really human. The result is one of the earliest Christian heresies, that Jesus *seemed* to be human, *appeared* to be human, but was really God. The name of the heresy is *docetism,* from the Greek word that means "to appear," "to seem." Many Christians—as well as many non-Christians—think that this is orthodox Christianity. But it is not.

Divinity belongs to the post-Easter Jesus, not to the pre-Easter Jesus. To think of the pre-Easter Jesus as divine actually diminishes him. If he was divine and had the power of God, then what he did wasn't all that remarkable. He could have done so much more. But the classic Christian affirmation about the pre-Easter Jesus is not that he was God, but that he was the decisive revelation of God. This is the cumulative meaning of the exalted language that Christians use for Jesus: in him, we see what can be seen of God in a human life.

Some of God's qualities cannot be seen in a human life. Consider for a moment the traditional attributes of God: omnipotence, omniscience, and omnipresence. Set aside for now whether these attributes make sense to you, and think about whether a human can reveal any of these. To say the obvious, a human cannot be omnipotent and still be human. A human cannot be omniscient, know everything, and still be human. What would it mean to imagine that the pre-Easter Jesus was omniscient—that he knew what was happening in China in his time? That he knew the theory of relativity? So also a human cannot be omnipresent, but can be in only one place at a time.

What can be seen of God embodied in a human life is God's character and passion. So, what do we see in the pre-Easter Jesus, understood as the revelation of God's character and passion? The quest for the pre-Easter Jesus, the historical Jesus, has been going on in scholarly circles for over two hundred years. It is complex and has yielded a wide range of results. But there are a number of "facts" that most scholars agree upon:

Jesus was Jewish and grew up in Nazareth, a peasant village in Galilee, the northern part of the Jewish homeland. Like the Jewish homeland as a whole, it was part of the Roman Empire.

Beyond that, we know nothing about his life until adulthood. Most likely in his twenties, he left Nazareth and became for a while a follower of John the Baptizer, a wilderness prophet who proclaimed the coming judgment of God.

After John was imprisoned by Herod, Jesus began his own public activity. He taught, healed, cast out demons, and attracted a following.

He spoke primarily to the peasant class. We know this because of the geography of his activity as reported in the Gospels. The powerful and wealthy elite lived mostly in cities. According to the Gospels, Jesus didn't go to cities, except to Jerusalem. His activity occurred in small towns, villages, hamlets, and the countryside, where the peasant class lived, mostly agricultural workers but also manual laborers.

He taught in parables and aphorisms. He was a storyteller and creator of memorable short sayings.

He was known (and criticized) for his association with marginalized people, often called "tax collectors and sinners" in the Gospels.

He was known (and criticized) for his inclusive meal practice. In a society where sharing a meal meant acceptance of those with whom one ate, he ate not only with peasants, but also with those commonly seen as outcasts, virtual untouchables.

At the center of his message was the "kingdom of God." In Mark, the earliest Gospel, the first words of Jesus are about the coming of the kingdom of God—Mark's advance summary of the gospel of Jesus. The kingdom of God is also central in Matthew and Luke. God's kingdom is not the afterlife; it concerns life on earth, as the Lord's Prayer emphasizes: "Your kingdom come . . . *on earth*" (see Chapter 24). The kingdom of God is what life would be like on earth if God were king and the kings and emperors of this world were not. It is a world where there's justice (everybody should have enough) and peace (no more war).

He taught nonviolent resistance to exploitation and violence. He did not teach, "Accept the way things are and wait for heaven," but sought to empower those who heard him to change the way things are.

In the season of Passover, he took his message to Jerusalem, the traditional center of the Jewish people. But in his time it was ruled by a high priest and aristocracy who owed their positions of power to Rome.

There he engaged in provocative actions: entering the city on a donkey, which symbolized that the kingdom of which he spoke was one in which there would be no war; indicting the Temple authorities for having made the Temple a den of robbers—collaborators with Rome and exploiters of the people; challenging the authorities and their representatives in a series of verbal conflicts; prophesying that Jerusalem and the Temple would soon be destroyed because, in words from Luke, Jerusalem did not know "the things that make for peace." (19:42)

Not surprisingly, he was arrested and crucified. Crucifixion was a Roman form of capital punishment, reserved for those who challenged imperial authority.

Of course, there is more that can be said about the pre-Easter Jesus. Many, many books have been written about him (including more than one by me).

But this concise summary is enough to enable us to entertain the question: If Jesus is the decisive revelation of the character and passion of God, as his followers have affirmed from the beginning, what does his life say about God?

In Jesus's compassion for the marginalized, for "the least of these," we see God's compassionate character. God wills the well-being of all of us, indeed, of all of creation. In Jesus's passion for the kingdom of God, we see God's passion for a transformed world—a world of justice and nonviolence in which no one needs to be afraid (see Mic. 4:1–4). God's character and passion as we see them in Jesus also have a confrontational dimension: they include the indictment of what gets in the way of the well-being of all of us, and of all that is.

## THE TITLES OF JESUS

We conclude by returning to some of the most important post-Easter titles of Jesus. All have meaning within a Jewish context, and all but the first also have a pointed meaning in the context of the Roman Empire.

*Messiah* (from Hebrew *mashiah*): Commonly rendered in English as "Christ," this title was distinctly Jewish and had no resonance in the Roman world. In a Jewish context, it referred to one *anointed* by God for a special role. In the Old Testament, it is sometimes used for the Jewish king. By the first century, it had acquired a narrower meaning within much of Judaism, referring to one promised and anointed by God to deliver the Jewish people from oppression and to bring in a new era on earth. There was, however, no unified messianic expectation among Jews in the time of Jesus. Some expected a warrior messiah. Some expected two messiahs—one a king and the other a priest. And some thought that God would bring in the new era without an intermediary. But to call Jesus the "Messiah," as his followers did, meant that they saw him as the one anointed by God to be the deliverer.

*Son of God:* In a Jewish context, the meaning of *Son of God* is shaped by the use of the phrase in the Old Testament. There it sometimes refers to Israel as a whole (Hos. 11:1), sometimes to the king (Ps. 2:7), sometimes to heavenly beings (Job 1:6, 2:1). Closer to the time of Jesus, it is used to refer to Jewish "holy men" who were mystics and healers. What all of these uses have in common is that the term refers to somebody in an especially intimate relationship with God.

In a Roman context—and recall that Jesus and his followers all lived within the Roman Empire—*Son of God* referred to the Roman emperor, from Caesar Augustus (emperor from 31 BCE to 14 CE) on. The title appeared on coins and inscriptions throughout the empire. Moreover, according to Roman imperial theology, Augustus (born Octavian) was the product of a divine conception, conceived in the womb of his mother, Attia, by the god Apollo. So when Jesus's followers spoke of him as the "Son of God," they were not only saying that he was intimately related to God (the Jewish meaning), but also directly challenging imperial theology's claim that Caesar was the "Son of God."

*Lord:* "Jesus is Lord" is the most widespread early Christian affirmation about him. Central to the letters of Paul, it is also common in the rest of the New Testament. In a Jewish context, *Lord* was a term used for God. It carried with it the notion of loyalty and allegiance. To say that "Jesus is Lord" means that he is the revelation of God to whom we are to be committed. In a Roman context, *Lord* (like *Son of God*) was one of the titles of the emperor. To affirm "Jesus is Lord" was to affirm that the emperor was not.

*Savior:* In a Jewish context, as we saw in Chapter 3, *savior* is associated with liberation from bondage (the exodus story), return from exile, rescue from peril, and much else. In a Roman context, *savior* was another title of the Roman emperor. Caesar Augustus was hailed as *savior* because he had brought peace on earth by defeating Mark Anthony and Cleopatra in the Battle of Actium in 31 BCE, thereby bringing the civil war that had raged for decades to an end. When early Christians spoke of Jesus as *savior,* they were contrasting two meanings of the word. Within Roman imperial theology, Caesar as *savior* meant one who brought peace through military victory and power. Jesus as *savior* meant one who brings peace on earth through justice and nonviolence.

Thus just as the pre-Easter Jesus challenged the domination system of his homeland, constituted by a combination of Temple authority and Roman imperial authority, so also the post-Easter Jesus of the developing tradition challenged the powers that ruled that world.

To deny that the pre-Easter Jesus was God does not diminish Jesus at all. Indeed, it exalts him. He was utterly remarkable—one of the two most remarkable people who ever lived. When I say this, I am often asked, "Who was the other one?" I answer, "I really don't care." My point is that the pre-Easter Jesus is a human possibility.

He is not special because he was divine and had a divine "boost" that we don't have. Rather, he was special because he was an utterly remarkable human being—like St. Francis with an exclamation point. Francis (1181/82–1226) is often seen as the most remarkable and Christlike of the Christian saints. Was Francis a human possibility? Yes. How often does a Francis come along? Not very often. Someone like Jesus doesn't come along very often either. The pre-Easter Jesus was extraordinary—so extraordinary that his followers saw in him the decisive revelation of God.

# CHAPTER 8

# The Death of Jesus

The death of Jesus is foundational to Christianity in a way that the death of no other religion's central figure is. Though Judaism, Islam, and Buddhism have stories about the deaths of their founders, these stories do not form the basis of their understanding of what it means to be Jewish, Muslim, or Buddhist.

But the death of Jesus has been crucial to Christianity from its beginning. Paul, writing earlier than the Gospels, proclaimed the heart of the Christian message to be "Christ crucified" (1 Cor. 1:23). All four Gospels climax with several chapters about Jesus's last week, death, and resurrection.

Jesus's death continues to be of major import for Christians today. Not only is it central to the whole of the New Testament, but it is highlighted in worship services, especially in language used in the Eucharist. So what is the death of Jesus about? Why did it happen? What did it mean? What does it mean?

## As Payment for Sin

The most widespread Christian understanding today is that Jesus paid the price for our sins by dying in our place. In theological language, this is called *substitutionary sacrifice, substitutionary atone-ment,* or sometimes the *satisfaction* understanding of Jesus's death. Jesus is the substitute who satisfied God's wrath by undergoing the punishment that we all deserve.

I absorbed this understanding as I grew up. "Were you there when they crucified my Lord?" asks a hymn. At the end of child-hood, my answer would have been, "Yes—I was there; my (and our) sins put Jesus on the cross." So also in the great twelfth-century hymn "O Sacred Head Now Wounded," which I still cannot sing without choking up, "Mine, mine was the transgression, but thine the deadly pain." The seventeen-century Protestant hymn "Ah Holy Jesus, How Hast Thou Offended?" asks, "Who was the guilty? Who brought this upon thee?" Its answer is, "I crucified thee."

So widespread is this understanding that many see it as or-thodox and traditional Christianity—both those who accept and defend it and those who criticize or reject it. Thus it is important to realize that it is not ancient, it is not in the Bible, and was not pres-ent during the first thousand years of Christianity.

Though language referring to Jesus's death as "for us" and as a "sacrifice" goes back to the New Testament, the *substitutionary* understanding of this language was first articulated in 1097 by Anselm of Canterbury. His book *Cur Deus Homo?* addressed the question: Why did God became human, incarnate in Jesus? His answer was that God's retributive justice requires that the penalty for our sins must be paid from the human side. But we are all sin-ners and thus cannot adequately make the payment. Only a perfect human can. But a human can't be perfect unless also divine. So God became human in Jesus in order to pay the price for our sins.

That this understanding of Jesus's death is not ancient does not in itself condemn it. Theological developments since the Bible can be illuminating and important. Revelation did not stop at the end of the biblical period. The Spirit of God continues to speak.

But this understanding has very serious problems, often unnoticed by Christians. First, by implying that Jesus had to die because of our sins and that this was part of God's plan to "save" us, it completely obscures and obliterates the historical meaning of his death. Historically, Jesus didn't just die—he was killed. And killed not by a criminal or assassin, but executed by established authority—a combination of imperial and collaborationist religious authority. Moreover, he was not just executed, but crucified—a form of Roman execution used for a specific class of offenders, those who systematically defied Roman authority, whether chronically rebellious slaves or leaders (and sometimes members) of resistance movements, violent or nonviolent. That means that the authorities didn't like what they had heard about Jesus. They saw him as challenging their established authority, and they knew he was beginning to attract a following.

So they killed him—in a very public way. If they had simply wanted to get rid of him, they could have killed him in a back alley or a cell. But they crucified him—a very public and prolonged form of execution deliberately designed to be seen and be a deterrent. It's message was clear: "This is what happens when you challenge us." But when Jesus's death is seen as part of God's plan so that our sins can be forgiven, all of this historical meaning disappears. Jesus's death is domesticated by obscuring the fact that he was killed by the powers that ruled his world. They killed him, but they didn't do it so that he could die for our sins.

Second, substitutionary sacrifice impugns the character of God. It portrays God as primarily punitive. Think of what this says about God. God is a lawgiver whose laws we have violated, and

God must enforce the law by punishing us unless an adequate sacrifice is made. Thus also the death of Jesus was part of God's plan; it was God's will that this immeasurably great and good person be executed. Sometimes this is "spun" in such a way to make God loving as well; namely, God loves us so such that he (and the masculine pronoun usually goes with this understanding) was willing to give up his only son to death on a cross. But even with that "spin," the punitive character of God dominates—somebody must pay the penalty. God requires blood—ours or the blood of Jesus.

Third, it distorts what Christianity is about. The substitutionary understanding of Jesus's death reinforces the widespread notion that Christianity is mostly about sin, forgiveness, believing that Jesus died for us, and a blessed afterlife. This understanding of Jesus's death is the foundation of the heaven-and-hell framework described in Chapter 1. But what if this isn't what Christianity is most importantly about? What if Christianity and salvation are really about transformation—the transformation of ourselves and of the world? Substitutionary understandings of Jesus's death obscure this. They make Christianity all about being forgiven by believing in Jesus so that we can go to heaven.

## THE MEANINGS OF JESUS'S DEATH

The Gospels and the rest of the New Testament ascribe several meanings to the death of Jesus. All of these are post-Easter. We have no reason to think that Jesus or his followers sought to find meaning in his death before it happened. To crystallize these meanings concisely:

*He was crucified.* In Paul's letters and the Gospels, this is a major emphasis. When Paul summarizes the gospel in a few words in 1 Corinthians, he reminds the community in Corinth that when he was with them, he proclaimed "Jesus Christ, and him crucified" (2:1–2; see also 1:23). A magnificent passage in Philippians also specifies the form of Jesus's death, "even death on a cross" (2:5–11). To emphasize in the world of the first century that Jesus was *crucified* signaled at once that this gospel was an anti-imperial gospel. So also in Mark, Matthew, and Luke when Jesus speaks three times of his upcoming death in Jerusalem (e.g., Mark 8:31–33; 9:30–32; 10:32–34), those predictions are never about his dying for our sins, but always about the fact that the authorities will kill him.

*Death and resurrection are dying and rising with Christ.* Within this understanding, the death and resurrection of Jesus became a metaphor for the personal and ultimately communal transformation at the center of the Christian life. We hear this in Paul's autobiographical comment: "I have been crucified with Christ; and it is no longer I who live, but it is Christ who lives in me" (Gal. 2:19–20). The old Paul has died; a new Paul has been born. In Romans, Paul speaks of dying and rising with Christ as the meaning of baptism (6:1–4). In Mark, Matthew, and Luke, Jesus, as he journeys to Jerusalem, invites, implores, commands that those who would follow him take up their cross, that is, embark on this path that leads to death and resurrection (e.g., Matt. 16:24). In the Gospel of John, a different image is used to make the same point, to be born again or to be born of the Spirit (3:3), which is to die to an old identity and way of being and to be born into a new identity and way of being. The death and resurrection of Jesus embody the path of personal transformation. This is also one of the core meanings of the season of Lent: to journey with Jesus from Galilee to Jerusalem, the place of death and resurrection—of transformation.

*Jesus's death is the revelation of the love of God.* This understanding has an important premise without which it doesn't make sense; namely, that Paul and other early Christians saw Jesus as the decisive revelation of God. In Jesus—in what he was like—we see what God is like. Thus, in Jesus's passion for the kingdom of God and his challenge to the powers at the risk of his own life, we see the depth of God's love for us. Note that in this understanding, it is not a punitive God who sends Jesus to die for our sins, but a God who is passionate about the transformation of the world.

## SACRIFICE

We return to the theme of sacrifice. *Substitution* seriously misunderstands the purpose and meaning of sacrifices in the Bible. They were never about substitution—as if those offering the sacrifice deserved to die, but God was willing to accept an animal as a substitute.

Most basically, *sacrifice* means to make something sacred by offering it up to God, as the Latin roots of the English word indicate: *sacrum* ("sacred") and *facere* ("to make"). An animal is offered up to God and becomes sacred in the process. Often within Judaism, the animal was cooked and then eaten by those offering the sacrifice, symbolically creating a meal with God, communion with God. God and the people consumed the same food. Gift and meal often go together in sacrifice.

Sacrifice in biblical times had many meanings, none of them about substitution. There were daily sacrifices offered by priests in the Temple; these were about "feeding" God, who dwelt there. There were sacrifices of thanksgiving; these were about gratitude—nothing was asked for. There were sacrifices of petition; here something was asked for, because people were in need—they were experiencing drought, famine, plague, war, personal misfortune, and so forth.

There were sacrifices of purification; these removed what was thought to be impurity. For example, after the birth of a child, a woman was considered impure for a period of time, and the impurity was removed by offering a sacrifice. But this was not about a sacrifice for sin—giving birth was not sinful. These sacrifices were about removing impurity, not about sinfulness. There were also sacrifices that dealt with the issue of sin or wrongdoing; one offered a sacrifice, a gift to God, to make amends, to heal the broken relationship. But even here the notion of substitution was not present.

Sometimes Christians think the "scapegoat," the second goat mentioned in connection with the ritual for the Jewish Day of Atonement, provides a model for Jesus's death as a sacrifice for sin. But in Judaism, the scapegoat was not sacrificed. Rather, the sins of the people were symbolically placed upon the goat, which was then driven into the wilderness (Lev. 16:20–22). The goat was a "sin-bearer"—but it was not killed, not sacrificed. Indeed, to have offered up a scapegoat laden with sin as a gift to God would have been a sacrilege.

Was Jesus's death a sacrifice in any of the particular ways suggested above? Not really, except for the theme of gift and meal, to which we turn later. But was it a sacrifice in the broader ancient meaning of the word, a meaning that continues into the modern world even in secular language? Yes.

Think of how we use the word. We say a person sacrifices his or her life for a cause or for another person. We commonly speak of soldiers sacrificing their lives for the sake of their country. If firefighters are killed in the process of rescuing people from a fire, we speak of their sacrifice. Even when a death is not involved, we sometimes speak of people sacrificing their lives for the sake of caring for others—in their family or in the larger world.

Sacrifice and love often go together. People who sacrifice their lives most often do so because of a greater love. Three twentieth-century Christian martyrs are exemplars of this combination of sacrifice and dying for others. Dietrich Bonhoeffer, a gifted and brilliant German Lutheran pastor and theologian, was executed for his involvement in the July 1944 plot to assassinate Hitler. His life was a sacrifice even before his death. And he died because of his love for the German people and those whom they were victimizing. Martin Luther King, Jr., sacrificed his life, because of his love for his people and his passion for the American dream. Oscar Romero, archbishop of San Salvador, was killed in 1980 by an assassin, because of his criticism of those in power who were oppressing the Salvadoran people. Did he sacrifice his life because of love for others? Yes.

Were any of these deaths substitutions? Of course not. So also we can speak of Jesus sacrificing his life, being willing to die because of his love for others, without in any way implying that

God required his death as a sacrifice so that we can be forgiven. It would be ludicrous to suggest that God required the deaths of Bonhoeffer, King, and Romero. No, they were killed because of their passion for a different and better kind of world. So also, Jesus sacrificed his life. He offered it up as a gift to God—not because God required it, but because he was filled with God's passion for the kingdom of God—a different kind of world.

# CHAPTER 9

# Easter

Easter is the most important Christian festival. It is also the most ancient, significantly older than Christmas. We do not know when it first began to be observed as an *annual* festival. In first-century Christian writings, there is no reference to a special once-a-year celebration. Moreover, the date for celebrating Easter varied considerably for a number of centuries and was not universally resolved until at least the 600s. But, though there seems to have been no annual celebration of Easter in first-century Christianity, the proclamation "God raised Jesus" was central to Christianity from the beginning. Indeed, celebrating Sunday as the "Lord's Day" reflects its importance.

Many—perhaps most—American Christians understand what happened at Easter as a "physical" event in which God miraculously transformed the corpse of Jesus, so that his tomb was found empty. "Empty tomb" and Easter go together. I call this a literal-factual understanding of Easter, naming its primary emphasis; the resurrection literally happened—it is a fact of history.

At least half of American Protestants belong to churches that insist on this understanding of Easter. It is consistent with their commitment to the Bible as the inerrant and literal Word of God.

The Bible says the tomb was empty, so it was indeed empty—and not because somebody stole the body, but because God raised Jesus. For many of these, the factuality of Easter proves that Jesus really was the Son of God. Also for many, Easter is the defeat of death—not just for Jesus, but for all who believe in him. Easter is thus associated with the possibility of an afterlife for the rest of us.

Many in nonliteralist churches also see Easter this way, or think they are supposed to. Most of us grew up with it, even if our churches didn't insist upon it. In worship every Sunday, we hear phrases like "He suffered death and was buried and on the third day he rose again" and "Christ has died, Christ is risen." It is the impression formed by the way we celebrate Easter. The Gospel texts on Easter Sunday always include the story of the empty tomb, suggesting that Easter begins with that. We sing "Christ the Lord is risen today." In the church of my childhood, we also sang "Up from the grave he arose," though it has been decades since I have heard that hymn.

Then, on subsequent Sundays, we hear stories of Jesus appearing to his followers, often in quite physical ways. They see him in visual form, sometime with physical, fleshy features. The risen Jesus invites Thomas to touch his wounds (John 20:27), eats a piece of fish (Luke 24:42–43), and cooks breakfast for his disciples on the shore of the Sea of Galilee (John 21:1–14).

When these stories and the story of the empty tomb are heard in a modern cultural environment in which language is most often taken literally, the natural impression is that Easter is a physical or at least semiphysical event in which God miraculously transformed the physical corpse of Jesus and brought him back to life.

This way of seeing Easter treats it as a "public" event in the sense that it could have been experienced by anybody who was there. If

Pilate had checked the tomb, he would have found it empty. If we had been there with a video camera when Jesus appeared and displayed his wounds to Thomas, we could have recorded it.

Many in nonliteralist churches have not encountered an alternative understanding of Easter, other than skepticism, and so they think the literal-factual understanding of Easter is the only option. Some of them have misgivings about it, and wonder if that's okay. Can you be Christian without believing that the tomb really was empty?

To illustrate how widespread this understanding of Easter is in Christian and secular culture today, recall the media attention focused a few years ago on the discovery in a first-century tomb in Jerusalem of a clay bone box (*ossuary,* to use the technical term) inscribed "James the brother of Jesus." For most Christians the discovery of the James Ossuary was interesting, but not surprising. If authentic (and its authenticity is strongly contested), it would have been the earliest attestation outside the New Testament to Jesus as a figure of history and to his having a brother named James. For these Christians, this simply confirmed what they already believed, that archaeology verifies that there really was a Jesus. For skeptics, it was strong evidence that Jesus really existed—that he isn't a made-up figure, as some from time to time have argued.

But the exciting and titillating reason this story got so much media attention was the possibility, suggested by those involved in the discovery, that perhaps the bones of Jesus had also been interred in an ossuary in the same cave. If that were true, what would that mean? If Jesus's bones were discovered, would that mean that the resurrection never happened? And should that mean the end of Christianity?

I don't imagine that his bones will be discovered—but it's an interesting and important question and directly relevant to what we think Easter is about. Is Easter intrinsically about an empty tomb—about something extraordinary happening to the corpse of Jesus? Would Christianity be invalidated if we found his bones?

## THE RISEN JESUS

As mentioned, some Easter stories speak of Jesus in quite physical ways. But others report that he appeared in ways that transcend the physical. He appears to the disciples in a locked room (by passing through the walls? John 20:19); as a stranger to two of his followers who do not recognize him for several hours, and when they do, he vanishes (Luke 24:13–35); and to Mary Magdalene, who also does not recognize him (John 20:14). Beyond the Gospels, the risen Jesus appears to Paul in a vision a few years after Jesus's death, long after his ascension as narrated in Acts 1. According to Paul and the book of Acts, there were many more visions.

These stories and reports suggest that when we speak of Easter, of the resurrection of Jesus, we are talking about something more than a singular spectacular factual event in the past. The resurrection of Jesus is about more than the corpse of Jesus.

The alternative way of seeing the meaning of Easter does not focus on whether something spectacular happened to Jesus's corpse. I am convinced that this question is a distraction. In a book of essays on Easter by multiple authors published some years ago, my chapter was entitled "The Irrelevance of the Empty Tomb."[1]

Rather than focusing on "what happened," this approach focuses on the *meaning* of the resurrection of Jesus in the New Testament. What did it *mean* for his followers in the first century to say that God raised Jesus from the dead? Believe whatever you want about whether the tomb was really empty, whether you are convinced it was or uncertain or skeptical—what did Easter mean to his early followers? The answer to the question of meaning is clear. In the Gospels and the rest of the New Testament, the resurrection of Jesus has two primary meanings: "Jesus lives" and "Jesus is Lord."

As briefly exposited in Chapter 7, the first meaning of Easter is that Jesus was not simply a figure of the past, but one who continued to be experienced as an abiding reality in the present. Such experiences happened not only in the first century. Many Christians in the centuries since have had experiences of Jesus—some in dramatic visions and mystical experiences, others in quieter ways. If we were to discover the bones of Jesus, would we then need to say that all of these Christians were mistaken?

Second, he was experienced not simply as a continuing presence, but as a divine reality, as "Lord," as "one with God." This feature distinguishes experiences of the post-Easter Jesus from other experiences of somebody who has died. Surveys suggest that about half of surviving spouses will have at least one vivid experience of their deceased spouse. Such an experience might lead them to wonder whether their spouse is still in some sense alive. But it would not lead them to conclude that their spouse was now both Lord and God.

But there was something about the experience of the risen Jesus that led beyond "Jesus lives" to "Jesus is Lord." "Jesus is Lord" means that Jesus has been vindicated by the God of Israel, the creator of heaven and earth, and raised to God's right hand. "Jesus is Lord" means the lords of this world, including the ruler of the empire that executed him, are not supreme. To affirm "Jesus is

Lord" systematically subverts all other lords, including the lords of culture.

Thus Easter is about much more than whether a spectacular miracle happened on a particular day a long time ago. It is also about much more than surviving death, for Jesus or for us. It is about who is Lord. Is God as revealed in Jesus Lord? Or is somebody or something else Lord?

All of the above is why I think the question of the factuality of the empty tomb is irrelevant. Focusing on the empty tomb reduces the meaning of Easter to a spectacular event in the past. It makes the resurrection of Jesus vulnerable to skepticism. Do things like this really happen? And only to Jesus? Can I be a wholehearted Christian if I have doubts about this?

This alternative way of understanding Easter sees the Easter stories as parables—parables about Jesus. That is, it understands these stories metaphorically. Parable and metaphor are about meaning. The story of the empty tomb means that death could not hold Jesus, could not stop what he had begun. The powers killed him, sealed him in a tomb. But that was not the end—he continued to be known, and known as Lord. The angels at the tomb ask the women who have come to anoint his body, "Why do you look for the living among the dead? He is not here, but has risen" (Luke 24:5). In other words, "You won't find Jesus in the land of the dead."

The stories of his appearances make the same point, and more. When Jesus appears to two of his followers on the road to Emmaus in Luke 24, he is experienced as a stranger who travels with them, and then is recognized as Jesus in "the breaking of the bread." In John 20, he appears to Thomas, who needed, yearned, hungered for his own experience of the risen Jesus, and also blesses those who have not had such an experience and yet believe. In John 21, the commands of the risen Jesus are "Feed my sheep" and "Follow me" (vv. 17, 19).

Would the parabolic meanings of these stories be invalidated if the tomb had not been empty? If we discovered the bones of Jesus, would that mean that Easter is not true? Is Easter about much more than something happening to the corpse of Jesus? According to the New Testament, it is. The powers killed Jesus. But that was not the end. Jesus lives and is Lord.

# CHAPTER 10

# Believing and Faith

The verb *believe* and the noun *faith* are used extensively in all forms of Christianity. "I believe" or "we believe" stands at the beginning of the creeds used by most Christians (see Chapter 22). Its close relative *faith* is especially important for Protestants. The Reformation of the sixteenth century emphasized that our relationship with God is primarily about faith: we are "saved by faith," not "by works." Ever since, Protestants in particular have spoken of *believing* and *faith* as foundational to being Christian. But the common meanings of these words in modern English are very different from their premodern and ancient Christian meanings.

When I have asked classes in college, university, seminary, and church settings about their associations with the word *believe,* I typically hear:

"There are some things you can know, and other things you can only believe."

"I use the word when I'm not sure. Like, if you asked me what the capital of Kansas is, and I can't remember whether it's

Wichita or Topeka, I might say, 'I believe it's Topeka'—but I wouldn't be sure."

"When I say 'I believe you' to somebody, it means that I believe they're telling the truth."

"Sometimes we use it when we're talking about the future—like, 'I believe the weather will be nice tomorrow,' or 'I believe we'll make it though this.'"

In the first example, knowing and believing are different. Believing is what you turn to when knowledge runs out. In the second example, believing reflects uncertainty and tentativeness. In the third example, believing is what you do when you think someone is telling you statements that are true. In the final example, it means not knowing for sure, but thinking that the probability is good.

When I ask how they hear *believe* used in religious contexts, their responses include:

"Believing is what you do when things in the Bible aren't very credible—like creation in six days, or a virgin birth, or walking on water. It's about taking seriously things you otherwise wouldn't."

"Believing is about believing that there is a God, even though the reasons for doing so are inconclusive."

"People use the word when they say the creed—I guess it means that they believe what the creed says."

"When I've been asked by some Christians, 'Do you believe in the Bible?' I think they're asking whether I believe that everything it says is true."

These meanings of *believe,* religious and nonreligious, are reflected in the most common dictionary definitions (italicized words are examples provided in the dictionaries):

*Oxford American:* "To accept something as true; feel sure of the truth of; accept the statement of someone as true: *he didn't believe her.* To have faith, esp. religious faith: *there are those on the fringes of the Church who do not really believe.* To hold as an opinion; think or suppose: *I believe we've already met; things were not as bad as the experts believed.*" (Note how "to have faith" and to "really believe" are equated in the second sentence. The first part of the last example expresses uncertainty, and in the second part some people—the experts—have believed incorrectly.)

*American Heritage:* "To accept as true or real. To credit with veracity: *I believe you.* To expect or suppose; think; to have an opinion. To have firm faith, especially religious faith." (Again, note how *believe* and "firm faith" are identified.)

*Random House Webster's:* "To have confidence in the truth, existence, reliability, or value of something; to have religious faith; to have confidence or faith in the truth of: *I can't believe that story.* To have confidence in the assertions of a person. To hold as an opinion; suppose; think: *I believe they are out of town.*" (Note that the first example defines having religious faith with a negative: "I can't believe that story." The second example means "I *think* they are out of town," which is different from "I *know* they are out of town.")

These definitions of the common meaning of *believe* share two important features. First, they define *believe* as believing *that*—believing *that* something, a statements or statements, is true, with varying degrees of certainty. Indeed, believing most often involves some uncertainty—if there were no uncertainty, the verb would be *know,* not *believe.* Second, in a religious context, they identify *believe* with *having faith.*

## Premodern Meanings

The modern meaning of *believe* is very different from its meanings from Christian antiquity until the seventeenth century.[1] In English, prior to about 1600, the verb *believe* always had a person as its direct object, not a statement. It did not mean believing *that* a statement is true, with varying degrees of certainty, but more like what we mean when we say to somebody, "I believe *in* you."

Note the difference the preposition makes. To believe *in* somebody is not the same as believing somebody. The latter refers to believing *that* what the person has said is true—*that* his or her statements are true. But "I believe *in* you" means having confidence in a person, trusting that person. In a Christian context, it meant having confidence in God and Jesus, trusting God and Jesus.

The meaning of *believe* prior to about 1600 includes more. It comes from the Old English *be loef,* which means "to hold dear." The similarity to the modern English word *belove* is obvious. To *believe* meant not only confidence and trust in a person, but also to hold that person dear—to *belove* that person. *Believing* and *beloving* were synonyms.

Thus until the 1600s, to *believe in* God and Jesus meant to *belove* God and Jesus. Think of the difference this makes. To believe in God does not mean *believing that* a set of statements about God are true, but to *belove* God. To believe in Jesus does not mean to *believe that* a set of statements about him are true, but to *belove* Jesus.

This meaning goes back to ancient Christianity. The Latin roots of the word *credo,* with which the creed begins and from which we get the word *creed,* means "I give my heart to." *Heart* does not refer simply to feelings, to emotions, though those are involved. Rather, *heart* is a metaphor for the self at its deepest level— a level of the self beneath our thinking, willing, and feeling. To whom do you give your heart, your self? To whom do you commit yourself? Whom do you belove? "Do you believe in me?" meant "Do you belove me?"

The difference between *believing that* and *beloving* is older than the creed. It is also in the Bible. In the New Testament, the author of the Letter of James writes:" You believe *that* God is one; you do well. Even the demons believe—and shudder" (2:19). The demons *believe that* God is one—but they do not *belove* God.

So also in the Gospels. When Jesus spoke about the great commandment, he did not say, "You shall believe *that* these statements about God are true." Rather, he said, "You shall *love* the Lord your God with all your heart, and with all your soul, and with all your mind, and with all your strength" (Mark 12:30; Matt. 22:37; Luke 10:27). The text goes back to the Old Testament. It is a quotation from Deuteronomy 6:5. For Christianity and its Jewish roots, believing is beloving, loving, God.

The modern meaning of *believe* is thus a major distortion of ancient Christian and biblical meanings. To put the contrast very concisely, it is the difference between:

> *Believing that* a set of statements about God, Jesus, and the Bible are true.

> *Beloving God*—and for Christians, this means beloving God as known especially in Jesus.

For some, perhaps a majority of American Protestants and some Catholics, the former is what "saves us." But does *believing that* a set of statements are true save us, transform us? Or is it *beloving* God as known in Jesus that saves us by transforming us? The questions are rhetorical. *Believing that* a set of statements are true has little transforming power. But *beloving* God as known in Jesus has great transforming power.

## FAITH

The fate of *faith* is similar. In modern English, this noun has acquired meanings that are quite different from its premodern meanings. Here are two sets of dictionary definitions of *faith:*

> *Oxford American:* "Strong belief in God or in the doctrines of a religion."

> *American Heritage:* "Belief that does not rest on logical proof or material evidence. Often in Christianity: the theological virtue defined as a secure belief in God."

*Random House Webster's:* "Belief that is not based on proof. Belief in God or in the doctrines or teachings of religion."

*Oxford American:* "A system of religious belief: the Christian faith."

*American Heritage:* "The body of dogma of a religion: the Muslim faith."

*Random House Webster's:* "A system of religious belief: the Jewish faith."

As already noted, *faith* is often identified with believing, as in the first set of definitions. In the second set it is a synonym for religion. "What faith are you?" means "What religion do you belong to?" But neither of these modern meanings is what faith meant in premodern Christianity. The ancient meanings are expressed by the Latin words *fidelitas* and *fiducia* and their Greek equivalents.

*Fidelitas* means "fidelity"—"faithfulness." Think of what faithfulness means in a human relationship. Though sometimes narrowly restricted to sexual behavior, it does not mean simply not straying, but has a positive meaning of commitment, loyalty, allegiance, and attentiveness to the relationship. So it is in our relationship with God; faith as fidelity does nor mean simply not going after other gods, but commitment, loyalty, allegiance, and attentiveness to our relationship with God—in a Christian context, to God as known especially in Jesus.

*Fiducia* means "trust." Faith in God is more than commitment, even as it is not less. It is also about deep trust in God. Here the opposite of faith is not infidelity, but "mistrust"—that is, anxiety. A passage from Jesus in the Gospels expresses this perfectly. As he invites his hearers to consider the birds of the air and how God feeds them and the lilies of the field and how God clothes them in gorgeous splendor, he asks them several times, "Why do you worry . . . you of little faith?" and concludes, "Therefore do not worry" (Matt. 6:25–34; Luke 12:22–32). "Little faith" and worry, anxiety, go together. Deep faith—as trust, *fiducia*—liberates us from anxiety.

Think of how free you would be if there were no anxiety in your life. This does not mean you would not have concern for others and passion for a different kind of world. But these are quite different from anxiety.

Think of how different faith as fidelity and trust, as *fidelitas* and *fiducia,* is from faith as believing a set of statements to be true. The latter can even increase anxiety. For example, if we believe that there is a final judgment in which we are sent to either heaven or hell, how could we not be anxious? Have I believed strongly enough or behaved rightly enough? But faith as faithfulness and trust eliminates that anxiety and frees us for transformation in this life.

Faith as faithfulness to God and trust in God is the product of a deeper and deeper centering in God. Faithfulness leads us to pay attention to our relationship to God—through such attention, we become even more deeply centered in God. Trust is the fruit of that deeper centering. It grows as we center more and more in God.

Faith as *fiducia* is trusting in the buoyancy of God. Søren Kierkegaard (1813–55), one of the most important nineteenth-century thinkers in religion and philosophy, said that faith is like floating in seventy thousand fathoms of water. Of course, no ocean is that deep, but his point is clear. If we are fearful and struggle as we float in an immeasurably deep body of water, we sink and drown. But if we trust that the water will keep us up, we float. The image goes back to the stories of Jesus walking on water (Matt. 14:25), stilling storms at sea (8:23–27), and inviting Peter to walk to him on the sea (14:28–29). Peter does—but after a few steps, he becomes afraid and begins to sink. He calls out to Jesus to save him. Jesus reaches out his hand to him, saying, "You of little faith, why did you doubt?" (14:31).

## CHRISTIAN FAITH AND BELIEFS

While writing this chapter, I received a letter from a former Protestant pastor in Scotland. He said, "I am not a fundamentalist. Indeed, I left the ministry because I could no longer believe central elements of Christian teaching and doctrine." He continued:

> I have read several of your books, including *The Heart of Christianity*. I am confused by what you say about "faith" as something different from belief—that faith is more a matter of the heart than the head. But is this right? Is it historically correct? Don't beliefs matter? Haven't Christians thought for a very long time that believing the right things matters? Haven't people been persecuted for centuries because they didn't have the right beliefs? Isn't it orthodox Christianity to say that believing is the road to salvation?

My response included a crystallization of what I have said in this chapter, that Christian faith is primarily about faithfulness to God and trust in God as known in Jesus. I also said:

> My point is not that "beliefs" don't matter. Beliefs matter very much. There are "bad" beliefs that can get in the way

of faith, and worse. Bad beliefs have too often been a source of intolerance, cruelty, injustice, violence, persecution, and barbarism.

So also "good" beliefs matter—they can help us to get rid of unnecessary intellectual stumbling blocks to being Christian, and, even more important, they can shape us into becoming more compassionate, just, and peaceful beings.

So beliefs matter. But we should not imagine that "believing the right things" is all that matters. Faith is a much deeper movement of the heart, of the self at its deepest level. Christian faith is allegiance to and trust in God as known in Jesus.

CHAPTER 11

# Mercy

The word *mercy* and its relative *merciful* are very familiar to Christians. Confessions of sin commonly beseech God to be *merciful,* as does the threefold appeal in the Kyrie: "Lord have mercy upon us, Christ have mercy upon us, Lord have mercy upon us." *Mercy* and *merciful* also appear frequently in English translations of the Bible.

The problem is the common meanings of *mercy* and *merciful* today. In contemporary secular and Christian usage, they presuppose a situation involving a power differential between two parties. Somebody with power stands in relation to an offender or victim. The former can decide to punish the latter or to reduce or forgo punishment. A governor shows mercy by commuting a death sentence to life in prison. A parent shows mercy by deciding not to punish a disobedient child. A soldier decides not to harm a captive.

This is the first meaning of *mercy* in contemporary dictionaries:

*Oxford American:* "Forgiveness shown toward someone whom it is within one's power to punish or harm. Example: 'The boy was begging for mercy.'"

*Random House Webster's:* "Kindly forbearance shown toward an offender, an enemy, or other person in one's power."

*American Heritage:* "Clemency, leniency."

This is also the meaning of *mercy* within the heaven-and-hell Christian framework. In its emphasis on sin as the central issue in our relationship with God, it says that we have offended God through our disobedience and deserve to be punished, so we appeal to God for mercy. This meaning goes with the punitive image of God's character; God is like a disappointed parent, a stern and even wrathful judge, and we deserve to be punished. Mercy is connected with forgiveness. God's mercy and God's wrath are opposites. Within this framework, mercy is good news. Who wouldn't prefer God's mercy to God's wrath? But understanding *mercy* as the opposite of punishment is a severe narrowing and reduction of meaning of the biblical and ancient Christian word.

Granted, sometimes *mercy* and *merciful* do appear in biblical contexts where the issue is sin and forgiveness. In such contexts, they are good translations. But because of the common meaning of *mercy* and *merciful* today, they are many times not good translations. Instead, the fuller meaning of the ancient words is better conveyed in English by *compassion* and *compassionate.*

Our understanding of *mercy* and *merciful* and *compassion* and *compassionate* matters greatly. What is at stake is how we see the character of God and how we are to live. Are we to be merciful (forgiving) as God is merciful? Or are we to be compassionate as God is compassionate?

## COMPASSION

The etymology of the word *compassion* is based on Latin roots that mean "to feel with"—to feel the feelings of another. The use of the word *feeling* might suggest that it is only an emotion. But it is more than a feeling; it includes acting in accord with that feeling. Thus we often speak of *deeds* or *acts* of compassion. Somebody who feels sorry for somebody else but does nothing about it would not be thought of as *compassionate*.

The linguistic associations of the Hebrew word commonly translated into English as *compassion* are rich. The Hebrew word is the plural of a noun that in its singular form means "womb." To be compassionate is to be womblike: life-giving, nourishing, perhaps embracing and encompassing. To be compassionate is to feel for another the way a mother feels for the children of her womb; she loves them, wills their well-being, and sometimes becomes fierce when their well-being is threatened. To say that God is compassionate, as the Bible often does, is to say that God is like this.

Unlike the common meaning of *mercy* today, *compassion* does not imply a situation of wrongdoing. Consider two different responses to the 2010 earthquake in Haiti: "We should show mercy on the Haitians" and "We should be compassionate toward the Haitians." Which is more accurate? Had they done something wrong and thus needed our mercy, our forgiveness? Or were they suffering and thus in need of compassionate care and compassionate acts?

Given the modern meaning of *mercy* and *merciful, compassion* and *compassionate* are much better words in many biblical contexts for speaking of the character of God and how we should be and act. In the book of Exodus, when the Israelites were still in bondage in Egypt, we are told that they groaned under their slavery and cried out. Their cry for help rose up to God. God heard their groaning and took notice of them (2:23–25). This is compassion— not mercy. They were not in slavery because they had sinned and needed forgiveness. The exodus story of bondage and liberation includes no indication that their slavery was the result of sin. They didn't need *mercy*. Rather, God heard their suffering and responded compassionately.

Compassion is a major theme in the Prophets, the second main part of the Old Testament. According to Abraham Heschel, one of the most influential Jewish scholars of the twentieth century for Christians, the prophets felt the *pathos* of God—God's feeling for the suffering of the many and God's passion for a different kind of world. For Heschel, the source of prophetic inspiration was their "empathy" and "sympathy" with the divine *pathos*.[1] The Greek roots of *sympathy* and *empathy* mean the same as the Latin roots of *compassion*—to feel the feelings of another and to act in accord with those feelings. God is compassionate—and those who love God are to be compassionate.

In many passages in the New Testament too, *mercy* and *merciful* are used when *compassion* and *compassionate* would be much better translations of what is meant. They often appear in contexts when the issue is not wrongdoing. Examples:

In the Magnificat, Mary's song in the first chapter of Luke, God's *mercy* (1:50) is associated with liberation from oppression, protection from enemies, and a world of peace. *Compassion* a much better word; the text does not suggest that the Jewish people were suffering oppression and violence because they had been sinful.

In Mark 10:46–52, a blind beggar beseeches Jesus to heal him. In most English translations, he cries out, "Have mercy on me." But the issue was not that he was sinful and needed forgiveness. He was blind and wanted his sight restored. *Compassion* is a much better word for what he wanted and received from Jesus.

In the parable of the good Samaritan (Luke 10:29–37), after Jesus tells the story, he asks which of the three—the priest, the Levite, or the Samaritan—did the right thing? In most English translations, the answer is, "The one who showed him mercy." But the man wounded and brutalized by thieves hadn't done anything wrong. *Compassion* is a better word than *mercy* for the way the Samaritan acted.

## *Compassion* Versus *Mercy*

Is God merciful and therefore we are to be merciful? Or is God compassionate and therefore we are to be compassionate? Consider the difference it makes in two familiar sayings attributed to Jesus, one from the Sermon on the Mount in Matthew and the other from the Sermon on the Plain in Luke. Most English translations read:

Blessed are the merciful, for they will receive mercy. (Matt. 5:7)

Be merciful just as your Father is merciful. (Luke 6:36)

Given the common modern meaning of *mercy* and *merciful,* these passages mean that we should forgive people who offend us just as God forgives us. That is an important message—the world would be a better place if forgiveness were more commonly practiced.

But for many of us, how often does the issue of forgiving other people come up? To speak for myself, it's been a long time since somebody sinned against me, so that I felt called to forgive that person. I am aware that forgiveness is an issue in the lives of people who have been sinned against, often in terrible and horrific ways. But in my experience, the need to forgive others because they have wronged me has been rare. How often have you felt the need to be merciful? The point is that the use of the words *mercy* and *merciful* narrows the meaning of these sayings significantly—they apply only occasionally.

Think how the meaning of these sayings changes if we substitute, as we should, the words *compassion* and *compassionate* for *mercy* and *merciful:*

Blessed are the compassionate, for they will receive compassion.

Be compassionate just as your Father is compassionate.

They are no longer simply about forgiving those who have offended us. Their meaning is far more comprehensive. Mercy is a reactive virtue; we are called to be merciful on those occasions when we have been wronged. Compassion covers a much larger area of life, indeed, all of life; we are to be compassionate.

Note the importance of the second saying in particular. It crystallizes theology (what God is like) and ethics (how we are to live) into a few words: God's character is compassion, and we are to be compassionate. We are to show compassion as God shows compassion. Compassion is much more than mercy.

I think of a homeless man I know in my neighborhood. I see him almost every day. He sells newspapers. I stop and visit briefly and buy a newspaper, even if I already have it (and then let him keep the newspaper). Am I being merciful to him, showing him mercy? No, he has not wronged me. Am I, in a small and very modest way, being compassionate? I trust that is so.

To return to the Kyrie with its threefold appeal to God to "have mercy upon us:" In times when we have a strong sense of having sinned, the common meaning of the word *mercy* can have deep meaning. But think of the larger meaning the Kyrie would have if it used the word *compassion* instead: "Lord, have compassion on us, Christ have compassion on us, Lord have compassion on us." Each time we say or sing it, we would be reminding ourselves of our need for God's life-giving and nourishing quality, reminding ourselves that this is the character of God. God is not primarily a threatening judge to whom we appeal for mercy, but a life-giving and nourishing reality who wills our well-being and the well-being of the whole of creation, just as a mother wills the well-being of the children of her womb. And we are reminding ourselves that this is how we should be.

# CHAPTER 12

# Righteousness

*Righteousness* and *righteous* occur hundreds of times in English translations of the Old and New Testaments. Sometimes they refer to God's character and passion: God is *righteous* and passionate about *righteousness*. Sometimes they refer to a human virtue: the righteous will flourish and the wicked shall wither.

The problem is that these words in modern English most often have a negative connotation. When I have asked Christian audiences about their associations when they heard the word *righteous,* some terms they used were *holier-than-thou, judgmental, condemnatory, hypocritical, priggish, legalistic, moralistic, full of themselves, pompous,* and *arrogant.* Their responses reminded me of a remark, which I think goes back to Will Rogers, about a man who was so righteous he was no damn good.

But in the Bible, *righteousness* and *righteous* are positive words. They are associated with "doing what is right." To say that God is righteous means God does "what is right." Moreover, God is passionate that we do "what is right." Righteous people are those who do what is right.

Sometimes the words are used to refer to individuals, and thus to individual virtue and behavior. For example, Noah is called "a righteous man" (Gen. 6:9; 7:1), and this is the reason that he and his family are saved from the great flood. Abraham bargains with God about God's resolve to destroy the city of Sodom. If Abraham can find fifty righteous people, fifty individuals who do "what is right," will God spare the city (18:24)?

This meaning is frequent in the Bible. In Psalms and Proverbs, as well as elsewhere, the "righteous" and the "wicked"—those who do what is right and those who do the opposite—are often contrasted. In Proverbs especially, the righteous are promised rewards: they will prosper (e.g., 15:6). (The books of Job and Ecclesiastes challenge this claim. Sometimes the righteous suffer and the wicked prosper. Doing "what is right" does not guarantee a nice comfortable life. The prosperity gospel is wrong.) In contexts like the above, *righteousness* is a quality of individuals or groups who do the right thing.

## RIGHTEOUSNESS AS JUSTICE

Very importantly, there is another primary meaning of words commonly translated into English as *righteousness* and *righteous*. This meaning is social and political, not just individual. It refers to the way a society is put together—its political and economic structure, its distribution of power and wealth and their effects on society, from the microcosm of the family to the macrocosm of nations and empires.

In these contexts, *righteousness* would be better translated *justice*. *Righteousness* and *justice* are so closely related in the Bible that they are often synonyms. Consider a passage from the prophet

Amos in the 700s BCE, two centuries after the establishment of a monarchy and aristocracy in Israel. The domination system Israel's ancestors had known in Egypt now operated within Israel itself. The rich and powerful had created a social system that benefited themselves, and the result was a huge gulf between rich and poor, powerful and powerless. The poor and powerless—most of the population—were virtually a slave class.

Speaking in the name of God and addressing the rich and powerful, Amos contrasts their worship of God with what God really wants:

> *I hate, I despise your festivals,*
> *and I take no delight in your solemn assemblies.*
> *Even though you offer me your burnt offerings and*
>   *grain offerings,*
> *I will not accept them;*
> *and the offerings of well-being of your fatted animals*
> *I will not look upon.*
> *Take away from me the noise of your songs;*
> *I will not listen to the melody of your harps.*
> *But let justice roll down like waters,*
> *and righteousness like an ever-flowing stream.*
>   *(5:21–24)*

Note the last two lines. What God wants, what God is passionate about, is justice and righteousness. These lines illustrate a frequent feature of biblical language known as *synonymous parallelism,* in which a second line repeats in slightly different language what the first line says. "Let justice roll down like waters" and "righteousness like an ever-flowing stream" are synonymous phrases. Justice and righteousness are not two different things, but the same thing. Justice is righteousness, and righteousness is justice.

Another example is in the fifth chapter of Isaiah, which begins with Isaiah's "song of the unfruitful vineyard," a poetic and parabolic indictment of the same domination system that Amos challenged. Isaiah invites his hearers to make a judgment about an unfruitful vineyard whose owner has lavished it with great care. It concludes:

> For the vineyard of the LORD of hosts
> is the house of Israel,
> and the people of Judah
> are his pleasant planting;
> God expected justice,
> but saw bloodshed;
> righteousness,
> but heard a cry! (5:7)

Note, as in Amos, that *justice* and *righteousness* are equivalent terms. The *cry* with which the indictment ends is the cry of the oppressed.

## THE MEANING OF JUSTICE

The realization that *righteousness* and *justice* are often synonyms in the Bible takes us only part way toward reclaiming the biblical meaning of these words. Like *righteousness* and *righteous, justice* in modern American English often means something quite different from its biblical meaning.

For many in America today, the primary meaning of *justice* is the criminal justice system. The responsibility of the Department of Justice is the enforcement of our nation's laws, and its head is spoken of as our nation's chief law enforcement official. Victims of crime often exclaim, "We want justice." This kind of justice is *retributive justice* or *punitive justice.* It prosecutes and punishes those who violate laws in order to maintain law and order. This form of justice is necessary. People living together in groups need laws and the fair enforcement of laws. It is impossible to imagine a large-scale society without a criminal justice system.

But *justice* in the Bible most often means much more than this, indeed something quite different. When the Bible speaks of God's passion for righteousness and justice, it does not mean that God's primary passion is the punishment of wrongdoers. True, some passages do threaten wrongdoers with judgment and condemnation. But often *justice* and *righteousness* refer to the way "the world," the social order that humans create, should be. It can be—and most often is—unjust, shaped by the wealthy and powerful in their own self-interest. God's dream, God's passion, is for a different kind of world. This kind of justice is not *punitive justice,* but *distributive justice*—the fair distribution of the material necessities of life.

God's passion for distributive justice is grounded in a theological affirmation that God created the world and it belongs to God. This is one of the central meanings of the Genesis creation stories. Psalm 24 affirms it with remarkable concision. Its first verse exclaims, "The earth is the LORD's and all that is in it." The earth and everything in it do not belong to us, but to God—not to some small percentage of us, not even to us as a species, but to God.

Distributive justice in the Bible as the fair distribution of God's earth is economic justice. In this context, what is "fair"? The Bible does not provide detailed economic policies, even though it contains some of the most radical economic laws in the history of the world. For example, every seventh year, the sabbath year, all debts are to be forgiven and all slaves are to be set free. Every fiftieth year, the jubilee year, all agricultural land is to be returned to the family of its original owners, without payment. These laws were intended to prevent the emergence of a permanently impoverished underclass. Put in the positive, everybody should have enough of the basic necessities of life. In the ancient world, these included food, shelter, and safety.

Moreover, and importantly, distributive justice is not charity. Charity is helping people in need. Charity is always good and will always be necessary. Distributive justice does not ask kings and emperors to increase their charitable giving. Rather, it asks about the way the system is structured. How is it shaped and whom does it benefit? Does it benefit some inordinately?

This meaning of *justice* runs throughout the Bible. In the time of the exodus, the Hebrew slaves were exploited and oppressed by the wealthy and powerful in Egypt. In the time of the monarchy in Israel, the prophets indicted the powerful and wealthy elite who had created Egypt within Israel; and in the context of the exile, prophets indicted Babylon, the imperial power that ruled their world.

The indictment of injustice continues in the New Testament. Jesus and Paul and other figures important in early Christianity stood against the Roman Empire because of its injustice and violence. Many of them were killed by the authorities—not because they advocated charity and taught individual righteousness and the way to heaven. People do not get martyred for that. Why would the authorities care? Rather, they were killed because those in power perceived their message and passion to be a threat to "the way things were"—that is, to the way the wealthy and powerful had structured the world to garner most of society's resources for themselves.

## *Justice* Versus *Righteousness*

The realization that *righteousness* often means *justice* matters greatly. Consider the following passages from the Sermon on the Mount in Matthew. In the NRSV and most modern English translations, the word *righteousness* is used. In each case, the NRSV translation is printed first, and then the verse is printed again with the word *justice* substituted for *righteousness:*

Blessed are those who hunger and thirst for *righteousness,* for they will be filled. (5:6)
Blessed are those who hunger and thirst for *justice,* for they will be filled.

Blessed are those who are persecuted for *righteousness.* (5:10)
Blessed are those who are persecuted for *justice.*

People are seldom persecuted for behaving in accordance with a strict individual moral code. But people are often persecuted because of their passion for justice. Here is another:

Unless your *righteousness* exceeds that of the scribes and the Pharisees, you will not enter the kingdom [of God]. (5:20)
Unless your *justice* exceeds that of the scribes and the Pharisees, you will not enter the kingdom [of God].

Are we to be more righteous than the scribes and the Pharisees—
more punctilious, more rigorous—than they stereotypically were?
Is that what this saying means? The saying is not about outdo-
ing the scribes and Pharisees in moral meticulousness; it is about
making every attempt to see that justice prevails. One more:

> Strive first for the kingdom of God and God's *righteousness*.
> (6:33)
> Strive first for the kingdom of God and God's *justice*.

Note how the kingdom of God and *righteousness* are linked. But
is striving for the kingdom of God and God's righteousness about
being "holier than thou"? The saying sounds very different with
*justice:* the kingdom of God seeks God's justice in contrast to
human injustice.

How we hear *righteousness* and *justice* also affects what we think
the gospel, the good news about Jesus, is. In the first chapter of
Paul's letter to Christians in Rome, the only letter Paul wrote to
people he didn't know in person, he crystallizes the gospel as "the
power of God for salvation to everyone who has faith. . . . For in
it the *righteousness* of God is revealed through faith for faith; as it
is written, 'The one who is *righteous* will live by faith'" (1:16–17).

Once again, *righteousness* and *righteous* are better translated as
*justice* and *just*. But does *justice* here mean punitive justice—that
God will punish people? If so, how can that be good news? Only
if *justice* means distributive justice can the gospel be good news—
namely, that God offers grace equally to everybody. For Paul,
this meant to Jews first, but also to Gentiles. God's distributive
justice—God's offer of grace—is for everybody. As a saying at-

tributed to Jesus puts it, God makes the sun rise on the evil and the good and sends rain on the just and unjust (Matt. 5:45).

Thus righteousness as justice tells us not only what we should seek, but also reveals the character and passion of God. Is God's character primarily punitive, and God's passion punishment of wrongdoing? Or is God's character primarily gracious and compassionate, and God's passion that the world be fair? Is it the righteous—those who are morally correct—who live by faith? Or is it the just who live by faith?

# CHAPTER 13

# Sin

*S*in is a very big word in heaven-and-hell Christianity. Within its framework of meaning, as we saw in Chapter 1, sin is the central issue in our life with God. We have sinned and need forgiveness, and Jesus's death provides the basis for our forgiveness.

This emphasis on sin as the central issue and forgiveness as our central need is very old, the product of the process of accommodating Christianity to dominant culture that began in the fourth century when the emperor Constantine adopted it. The result is that sin became the primary metaphor for describing the human condition, the human predicament. Given that problem, what we need most of all is forgiveness.

Much of this chapter is a critique of what happens when the multiple and powerful biblical metaphors are reduced to sin as the one dominant metaphor, the "macro-metaphor," for what ails us. Because of this chapter's critical edge, I emphasize at the outset that sin matters. It is one of the Bible's major metaphors for the human condition, but it is one of several, not the only one.

So the question is not, "Does sin matter?" It does. And, crucially, it matters how we think of sin. Is it the macro-metaphor in our understanding of our life with God? If so, how has that affected our life with God? What do we think *sin* means, in both singular and plural form? What is *sin* and what are *sins*?

## DEMOTING SIN

Sin needs to be demoted from its status as *the* dominant Christian metaphor for what's wrong among us. As noted above, it is not the only biblical image for the human condition, but one of several. Moreover, it is not the primary one, not the most important one, not even a first among equals. Rather, it is a peer among several major metaphors. Demoting sin enables us to see the power and importance of the other metaphors. Ultimately it also enriches our understanding of sin.

In the story of what led to Israel's bondage in Egypt, sin is not an issue at all. The ancestors of the Jewish people were not in slavery because they had sinned. As slaves, what they needed was not forgiveness, but liberation. Imagine that the story offered them forgiveness, but left them in bondage. That would be a very different story.

In Israel's experience of exile in Babylon, sin does play a part. Some biblical texts say that the exile happened because of sin. But sin is not the primary image used for their predicament—exile was their problem. Forcibly removed from their beloved homeland, taken to an alien land named Babylon and controlled by their conquerors, they lived constricted and impoverished lives, virtually as slaves. What they needed was not primarily forgiveness (though that is present in the story), but a path out of exile, a way to return "home." It meant leaving Babylon and journeying on the way through the "wilderness," much of it desert. Is sin the primary metaphor in this story? No. If our problem is exile, we need a path of return—we need "the way of the LORD," as Isaiah 40:3 puts it.

This phrase from Isaiah, with its resonances of exile and return, is used by Matthew, Mark, and Luke as they introduce their stories of Jesus; "the way of the LORD" is one of their crystallizations of what the story of Jesus is about. The image is found in what may be the best-known parable of Jesus, the prodigal son (Luke 15:11–32). The younger son goes to "a distant country"—he becomes an exile. In exile, his life becomes so miserable that he finally "comes to himself" and resolves to return, to journey back to his father. Though the son prepares a confession of sin, the father doesn't need to hear it—indeed, the father sees the son a long way off and, filled with compassion, rushes out to meet him.

This parable is not a story about sin and forgiveness. Think of how different the story would be if the son had received forgiveness in exile and yet remained in a distant country working for a pig farmer. Nothing had changed—except that he had been forgiven and felt better. Would anybody bother to remember a story like that? Rather than being a story about sin and forgiveness, it is about exile, return, welcome, and celebration.

Yet another biblical image for the human condition is infirmity in its manifold forms: illness, blindness, paralysis, a bent and burdened back, deafness, woundedness. What the infirm need is not forgiveness, but healing and wholeness. As John 9 says in the story of Jesus healing a blind man, the infirm are not infirm because they or their parents sinned. Infirmity is not about sin—and thus forgiveness would miss the point.

When sin becomes the "one size fits all" metaphor for the human condition, it obscures the rich and important meanings of these other metaphors. According to the Bible, our predicament—

what we need deliverance from—is not simply or primarily sin. There are other issues such as bondage, exile, blindness, infirmity, hard-heartedness, and so forth. For these, forgiveness is not the answer. People in bondage need liberation from the Pharaohs who rule their lives, people in exile need to leave Babylon and return home, people who are blind need to see, people who are sick or wounded need healing, people who are outcasts need community. But the heaven-and-hell Christian emphasis on sin and forgiveness casts these meanings into shadow, eclipsed by sin.

## Sin and Sins

In the Bible and in postbiblical Christianity, the term appears in both singular and plural forms: *sin* and *sins*. When used in the plural, it most often means particular failures such as disobedience to God's will and infractions against God's commands. Some Christians understand this as "missing the mark," with the "mark" understood as God's commands. We "miss the mark" by disobeying God's commands again and again. When this is the case, forgiveness is the imperative need.

This understanding commonly goes with the individualization of sin—that sins (plural) are acts of wrongdoing committed by individuals. Of course, it is true that we as individuals do commit sins and "miss the mark." But this focus on sin as the wrongful acts of individuals misses the fuller and richer biblical meanings of *sin*. The Bible does speak about sin as something that individuals do. But it also speaks about, to use modern language, institutionalized sin, systemic sin, sin built into the structures of society. There is collective corporate sin.

In Micah 1:5 the prophet rhetorically asks what the transgression of Jacob, the northern kingdom, Israel, is? His answer is that the sin of Israel is Samaria. And the sin of Judah, the southern kingdom? It is Jerusalem. Sin as cities? Samaria and Jerusalem were the capitals of the northern and southern kingdoms and thus the centers of monarchy and domination. The ruling elite had built sin into the very structures of society. This is sin as systemic injustice and systemic violence. Do the elite need forgiveness for this? Yes. But what is also needed is a change in the system.

Sin in the singular is also used in the Bible to refer to a power that holds us in bondage. Here sin is not primarily about individual acts of wrongdoing, but refers to a power that rules us—a Pharaoh within who controls us and refuses to let us go.

Paul writes eloquently about sin as a power in Romans 7:7–24:

> Sin . . . produced in me all kinds of covetousness. . . . Sin . . .
> deceived me. . . . I do not understand my own actions. For I
> do not do want I want, but I do the very thing I hate. . . . It
> is no longer I who do it, but sin that dwells within me. . . . I
> can will what is right, but I cannot do it. For I do not do the
> good I want, but the evil I do not want is what I do. Now if
> I do what I do not want, it is no longer I who do it, but sin
> that dwells within me.

"It is no longer I who do it" is not meant as an excuse. Rather, it is a recognition of what many people know in their own experience, that we are often not free, but captives. When sin is bondage, as it is here, the remedy is not forgiveness, but liberation from bondage.

The nature of sin in the singular has been insightfully named in various ways by Christian thinkers over the centuries. One influential stream of Christian wisdom understands the root of sin (from which sins in the plural flow) as *hubris,* a Greek word commonly translated into English as "pride." "Pride" is somewhat misleading, because in ordinary usage today pride can sometimes be good or at least okay. When a person says, "I felt proud of myself when I . . ." (fill in the blank), that might be fine. Many people suffer from low self-esteem, and thus sometimes feeling good about oneself is good.

But *hubris* means much more than this. It means puffing oneself up to inordinate size—attempting to become godlike. It means making oneself the center of the universe and the center of one's concern. This is characteristic not only of world conquerors and extreme narcissists. It is the universal—or at least virtually universal—product of normal human development. Early in the process from infancy into childhood and adulthood, we become aware of the self–world distinction—that the self and the world are separate. This is the birth of self-awareness. All of us experience this. The natural result (meaning virtually inevitable, and perhaps completely so) is self-concern. The world is not only separate from us, but not completely reliable, even dangerous. And so we become focused on the self and its well-being. This happens to all of us.

*Hubris* infects not only individuals, but also groups, countries, and humanity itself. Groups often puff themselves up to inordinate size, overestimating their own importance and causing conflict in society because they believe they have a monopoly on the truth. Countries do too—think of the total allegiance they sometimes demand. And empires do—the fatal flaw that causes the downfall of empires is overreaching themselves, imagining that their power and control are invulnerable. They imagine there is nothing they cannot do. *Hubris* is also a characteristic of humanity as a whole, as the ecological crisis has made us aware. For millennia, we have imagined ourselves to be the center and climax of creation; we have treated the earth as if it belongs to us, as if the nonhuman world is there solely for our own benefit. All of this is *hubris*.

*Hubris* is a powerful image for sin in the singular. It accounts for many and perhaps all sins in the plural, which stem from self-concern and concern for the security of the self, on both the individual and social level. A primary concern with the well-being of one's group or country often leads to injustice and violence.

A second image of the root of sin initially seems like its opposite—sin not as *hubris,* but as sloth. But they are not incompatible opposites; rather, they are complementary. In a metaphor that I owe to one of theologian Harvey Cox's many perceptive books, sloth means "leaving it to the snake." The reference is to Adam and Eve in the Garden of Eden letting the serpent tell them what to do. Within the framework of this metaphor, their sin was not *hubris,* not puffing themselves up to inordinate size, but slothfully and complacently accepting what the snake told them to do. Sin as sloth is letting others decide your life for you. You are "going along" with what you have heard, with how things are. Like *hubris,* sloth is a root sin (singular) from which sins (plural) proceed.

When *hubris*—centering on the self—is the problem, forgiveness is not the solution, or at least not an adequate remedy. A person brutally or miserably afflicted by self-centeredness can be forgiven and feel forgiven and still be unchanged, still a prisoner of *hubris.* So also with sloth. The remedy for *hubris* and sloth is a recentering of the self—we need to center ourselves in God, not in our own concerns or the lords or powers who rule this world.

Centering in God is "the way of the LORD," the path of return, liberation, and wholeness.

Another very important root image for sin in the Bible is idolatry. In Christian usage, it has several meanings, some of which distort and trivialize it. For some Christians, it means the gods of other religions. "Their gods are idols; our God is the true God." Sometimes among Protestants, idolatry has been associated with Catholics and the presence in their churches of statues and "graven images" of people other than Jesus, especially Mary and the saints. In the church in which I grew up, we took it for granted that Catholics were idolatrous because of their prodigal use of images. Indeed, they even prayed to Mary and the saints.

But none of this expresses the biblical meaning of idolatry. Idolatry is a matter of lordship. Who is your lord, the center of your allegiance? Yourself and those whom you love most dearly? Your group or your country? Humanity? Or God, who is more than all of this? Idolatry occurs when we make anything less than God the center of our lives. It encompasses both *hubris* and sloth. It is centering in something other than God and letting something other than God's passion shape our lives.

From idolatry as centering in the finite flow sins plural. Hence the great commandment in both the Old and New Testaments: "You shall love the Lord your God with all your heart, and with all your soul, and with all your mind, and with all your strength" (Mark 12:30; Matt. 22:37; Luke 10:27; Deut. 6:5).

This more comprehensive understanding of sin is rich. It names what commonly ails us. At the same time, it does not become the "one size fits all" description of us. For some people—indeed the majority of people who have ever lived—the issue is not so much that they sinned, but that they were sinned against. There are victims of sin as well as sinners. Victims of sin need not forgiveness (though they may need to forgive), but liberation, reconnection, healing, wholeness, and a world of justice and peace. All of this is central to God's passion in the Bible as revealed decisively in Jesus.

Within this broader biblical understanding of sin, forgiveness is not the primary antidote to sin. Rather, the primary antidote is a deeper and deeper centering in God rather than centering in the self (*hubris*) or the lords of this world who tell us how to live (sloth). Both are forms of idolatry. The antidote is the opposite of idolatry: "You shall love the Lord your God."

## A Modest Proposal

Christian language and liturgy need to speak not just about sins in the plural and our need for forgiveness. They also need to speak about sin as a power that holds us in bondage. They need to speak about the Pharaohs who rule our lives, the Babylon in which we live as exiles, the self-concern that dominates us, the blindness and limited vision that is the natural product of growing up in a particular time and place. They need to speak about the ways we have wounded and been wounded and our need for transformation and healing.

But these other images of our predicament and our need are largely absent from contemporary Christian worship. In most churches, liturgical and nonliturgical, the issue is sin, understood primarily in the plural as infractions committed against God and our neighbors. In liturgical churches, a "confession of sin" and "absolution" (the pronouncement of forgiveness) are a standard part of worship. In nonliturgical churches, most of which are "conservative," there may not be a standardized confession of sin and absolution, but it is still clear that sin is the central issue in our life with God. Our sins are the reason Jesus had to die.

Imagine the difference it would make if Christian worship services also highlighted the other biblical images for what ails us. Imagine Christian liturgies and preaching that emphasize that we are Pharaoh's slaves in Egypt and need liberation, that we are exiled in Babylon and need a path to return home, that we are blind and need to see again, that we are sick and wounded and need healing and wholeness. And, yes, that we are sinners who need forgiveness.

Imagine—to become more specific than I wish to be—that a confession of sin and absolution were part of the liturgy one Sunday out of five. Imagine that on the other four Sundays, the confession of sin were replaced by images of our predicament as bondage, exile, blindness, and infirmity. Imagine the absolution replaced by the proclamation that God wills our liberation from bondage, our return from exile, our seeing again, our healing and wholeness.

Sin matters. But when it and the need for forgiveness become the dominant issue in our life with God, it reduces and impoverishes the wisdom and passion of the Bible and the Christian tradition.

# CHAPTER 14

# Forgiveness and Repentance

L ike sin and because of sin, forgiveness is also a dominant theme in most understandings of Christianity. With good reason. Whenever sin is emphasized, forgiveness invariably is as well, for it is the antidote to the most common understanding of sin. Moreover, whenever Christians recite the Lord's Prayer, the best-known prayer in the world, forgiveness is mentioned. And petitioning God for forgiveness and mercy is part of most worship services.

Most often (invariably?) a primary emphasis on our need for forgiveness goes with a punitive image of God's character. God might punish us, indeed will punish us, in this life or the next, if we haven't sought and received forgiveness.

This notion was widespread in the world of my childhood, and I suspect it still is to some extent. I recall serious discussions about whether suicide was an unforgivable sin. The logic was that you can't repent if you're dead because you committed suicide. Suicide can't be forgiven. The logic was sometimes taken further. Suppose you didn't commit suicide, but nevertheless died with sins that hadn't been forgiven? If you died with unforgiven sins, might you go to hell?

I suspect that at least a majority of people today think this is a bit extreme. Would you really be eternally punished because of sins unforgiven since your last confession? But that possibility haunted the psyches of many and maybe most Christians for centuries. What happened if you died suddenly of illness or were killed and weren't in a state of grace, that is, forgiven? Being forgiven was the way into eternal life.

But what happens if we understand forgiveness in a different Christian framework—one that does not emphasize the punitive character of God, but the gracious character of God? Suppose that God is gracious and forgiving, compassionate and loving, passionate about our transformation and the transformation of the world. Within this framework, this context, what does forgiveness mean? In our relationship to God? And in our relationships with people?

## FORGIVENESS IN RELATION TO GOD

Do we need to be forgiven by God? Well, it all depends upon what you mean by that. Do we imagine forgiveness as something God decides to do—that God decides to forgive some people, but not others? If so, what is the basis for being forgiven by God—are some among the elect (chosen by God) and others not?

In the Bible, the yearning for forgiveness by God sometimes comes as the result of committing violations of God's commands. Some biblical texts are filled with a woeful sense of wrongdoing. When a strong sense of guilt is the issue, forgiveness is the answer.

But is being forgiven by God dependent on something we do? Some believe we can be forgiven only if we earnestly confess our sins, believe in Jesus, and resolve to live differently. But what do we do if we fail again? Seek forgiveness again? If so—and this is a very common way of thinking—then forgiveness is conditional. We can be forgiven only *if*... (fill in the rest of the sentence).

Or are we already forgiven—that is, accepted by God, loved by God—whether we know that or not? This has been the radical meaning of forgiveness and grace in the Bible and influential theological voices within the Christian tradition. For Luther, this discovery was the experience that led to his understanding of radical grace and his deliverance from what was for him an agonizing search for God's approval.

A very powerful expression of this in modern times is in a book of sermons by Paul Tillich, one of the most influential mainline Protestant theologians of the twentieth century.[1] The sermon's title is "You Are Accepted." Its theme, sounded again and again, is we are forgiven, accepted by God, in spite of all that we think separates us from God. God's love, God's grace, God's forgiveness, God's acceptance of us is unconditional. Grace means that God's love is a given.

This is forgiveness "in spite of"—that is, a sense of being accepted by God in spite of our imperfections and worse. Have I been less than I could and should be? Less loyal, less committed, less attentive, less generous, less willing than I should be to spend and be spent for the sake of what it means to follow Jesus? Yes. And God's forgiveness, God's mercy, means that I am loved by God in spite of that? Yes.

Of course it is vital that we see that, realize that, make it real by internalizing it, or else nothing will change in our lives. If we don't see that, we will continue to feel guilty and alienated from God. We will continue to focus on what we must do to be saved.

But if we do see that forgiveness is unconditional and realize it by making it real, then the Christian life no longer consists of believing or doing what we must in order to be forgiven. God already accepts us and wills our well-being. See this, believe this, realize this, and your life will change. You will no longer be preoccupied with becoming secure by measuring up.

This is the intended meaning of the proclamation of God's forgiveness in the absolution that follows the confession of sins in liturgical churches. The absolution proclaims that we are forgiven and accepted by God. It thereby also poses the question: Whose verdict of ourselves are we going to accept? Our own? Our culture's? Our church's? Or God's? And if we are already accepted by God, beloved by God, then what is the Christian life about? If the Christian life is not about measuring up, then what is it about? It is about liberation from that concern so we can participate in God's passion for transformation—of ourselves and the world.

## FORGIVENESS IN HUMAN RELATIONS

Forgiveness occurs not only in our relationship with God, but also in our relationships with one another. To begin with an obvious example, parents know that forgiveness is part of raising children. Did the children have accidents during toilet training? Yes. Were they sometimes willful? Yes. Were they sometimes troublesome in adolescence? Yes. But good parents continue to love them. This is forgiveness as unconditional love, even as it wants something better for the beloved.

Forgiveness also takes place in our relationship to our own past. How much do our memories of difficult years continue to enslave us? Forgiveness of those in our past is a way of becoming free from the bondage of those wounds.

Forgiveness is also an important element in adult relationships, for some people more than others. I have been fortunate in my adult life. I have seldom experienced situations in which I felt that somebody had wronged me, sinned against me, so that forgiveness was called for. It hasn't come up for me for years at a time.

But I also know that many in adulthood have experienced brutality, betrayal, callous and consistent insensitivity, and injustice in social groups, whether in the family, at work, or in society as a whole. For them, the ability to forgive may need to be cultivated. And the experience of forgiveness may be a crucial issue for those who have done grievous wrong. Perhaps the best-known large-scale example of this in recent years is the Truth and Reconciliation Commission in South Africa in the years immediately following apartheid.

In a setting like this, what does it mean to forgive? Is it simply saying, "It's okay"? Or is it about making one's peace with the past, so that one can move into a new way of life that involves freedom from that past. Is liberation without forgiveness possible?

## REPENTANCE

Repentance is most commonly associated by Christians with sin and forgiveness. When we have sinned, we are to repent of our sins so that we can be forgiven. Some Christians (including me as I was growing up) believe that forgiveness doesn't happen apart from sincere repentance. Without repentance, there is no forgiveness. Within this framework, repentance means being thoroughly sorry for our sins and earnestly resolving not to continue the behaviors and thoughts understood to be sins. And if our repentance doesn't contain enough of that remorse and resolve, can we be forgiven?

This understanding of repentance also affects the practice of forgiveness in human relationships. If somebody who has wronged me says, "I'm sorry," and I'm not sure if that person really means it, am I still supposed to forgive?

This common linkage between sin, repentance, and forgiveness has affected Christian understandings of the season of Lent. Lent—the forty days leading up to Holy Week, Good Friday, and Easter—is a "penitential" season in the Christian liturgical calendar, observed by most Christians, though not by some Protestants (I continue to be surprised when I meet Christians who have never heard of Lent). As a season of "penance," Lent is a time for thoughtful consideration of our lives and our sins. Sometimes it involves giving up something for Lent. It is a somber season of contrition and preparation for Jesus's dying for our sins on Good Friday. Lent and Holy Week are about sin, repentance, and forgiveness.

The biblical meanings of repentance are quite different and much richer. It has two primary meanings. The first flows from the Hebrew word in the Old Testament commonly translated into English as *repent* or *repentance*. It means "to turn, to return." The word directly relates to ancient Israel's experience of exile in Babylon. To *repent* meant "to return"—to embark on a journey of return to the "homeland," the Holy Land, where God is. That is the metaphorical meaning of the Holy Land, Jerusalem, Zion, the Temple—all are symbols for the presence of God. To repent is to embark on a journey of return to God—a journey that is also with God.

*Repentance* is a main theme in the New Testament as well. In Mark, the first Gospel to be written, in Jesus's inaugural address, his first words in any Gospel, Jesus proclaims "The kingdom of God has come near; *repent,* and believe in the good news" (1:15). The word continues to have its Old Testament resonance: return from exile, turn and return to God, embark on "the way of the LORD."

It also has a second resonance that flows from the roots of the Greek word in the New Testament commonly translated into English as *repent* or *repentance*. Its Greek roots mean "to go beyond the mind that we have." The phrase is both provocative and evocative. This is what repentance means?

And what does it mean to "to go beyond the mind that we have"? This is the evocative part. The mind that we have is the mind acquired by being socialized in our particular place and time. The natural result of growing up is to have an enculturated mind, a way of seeing shaped by what we have learned. Few if any of us escape this. So to go beyond the mind that we have means seeing in a new way—a way shaped by God as known decisively in Jesus. This is repentance.

The Bible does speak of repenting for our sins. But the emphasis is not so much on contrition and sorrow and guilt, but about turning from them and returning to God. Repentance is about change, not primarily a prerequisite for forgiveness. To repent means to turn, return to God and to go beyond the mind that we have and see things in a new way. That's pretty exciting.

Forgiveness is not dependent upon repentance. We are forgiven already, loved and accepted by God. We don't need to do anything to warrant God's love. But repentance—turning and returning to God, going beyond the mind that we have—is the path that leads to transformation.

# CHAPTER 15

# John 3:16

John 3:16 is probably the best-known verse in the Bible. In the familiar form in which I memorized it more than sixty years ago: "For God so loved the world that he gave his only begotten son, that whosoever believes in him should not perish but have everlasting life" (KJV).

For many Christians, this verse is the most concise summary of the Christian gospel. "John 3:16" often appears on homemade signs held up by fans behind the goal posts as football teams attempt to kick a field goal or the point after a touchdown.

It is easy to understand why. Understood within the framework of heaven-and-hell Christianity, it expresses the heart of what the heaven-and-hell framework affirms:

*For God so loved the world:* This expresses a main Christian conviction that God loves the world. It is how the rest of the verse is understood that gives it its distinctive meaning within the framework of heaven-and-hell Christianity.

*That he gave his only Son* (or in some translations, *his one and only son*): This is understood to mean both that Jesus is the only

Son of God and that God gave him to die for the sins of the world. The "giving of the Son" means that Jesus died in our place, so that we can be forgiven.

*So that everyone who believes in him:* What we need to do is to believe in Jesus as God's only son and as the one who died for us. This is the path of salvation.

*May not perish but may have eternal life:* The consequence of believing in Jesus is survival of death and everlasting life, meaning heaven.

To say the obvious, note how this understanding of the verse sounds the main themes of the heaven-and-hell Christian framework: we are saved (that is, get to go to heaven) by believing that Jesus is the only son of God, who died for our sins. Notice also how this puts a condition on the opening line "For God so loved the world"; namely, the love of God is conditional. Though God loves the world, only those who believe in Jesus will be saved. In extreme form (not all that uncommon), the verse means that God loves you, but God will send you to hell and eternal torment if you don't believe in Jesus. But all of this is a significant misunderstanding of what John 3:16 means in the context of John's Gospel.

*For God so loved the world:* In John, as in the New Testament generally, *world* has two quite different meanings. One meaning is positive: the *world* is the world created by God—the whole of creation. The other meaning is negative: the *world* is "this world," meaning the humanly created world of cultures with their domination systems. In John and in Paul, "this world" rejected Jesus.

But God loves the divinely created world—not just you and me, not just Christians, not just people, but the whole of creation.

*That he gave his only Son:* John's Gospel does not include the notion of substitutionary sacrifice; indeed, none of the Gospels do. The *giving* of the Son in John refers to the incarnation as a whole and not primarily to the death of Jesus. How much does God love the world? So much that God was willing to become incarnate in the world.

*So that everyone who believes in him:* The premodern rather than modern meaning of *believe* is intended. In this verse, as in the Bible generally, *believe* does not mean believing theological claims about Jesus, but *beloving* Jesus, giving one's heart, loyalty, fidelity, and commitment to Jesus. This is the way into new life.

*May not perish but may have eternal life: Eternal life* is commonly understood to mean a blessed afterlife beyond death. But in John's Gospel, it is a present experience. The Greek words translated into English as *eternal life* mean "the life of the age to come." Within John's theology, this is still future and to be hoped for. But it is also present, something that can be known, experienced now. Consider John 17:3: "This is eternal life, that they may know you, the only true God, and Jesus Christ whom you have sent." Note the present tense. This *is* eternal life (the life of the age to come); and its content is *knowing* God and Jesus. To know God and Jesus in the present is to participate already in the life of the age to come.

Thus in John, this verse is not about believing a set of statements about Jesus now for the sake of heaven later. It is about beloving Jesus and beloving God as known in Jesus, in the incarnation, and entering into "the life of the age to come" now. It is not about people going to hell because they don't believe. It is about the path into life with God now.

# CHAPTER 16

# Born Again

For millions of Christians, *born again* is a completely positive phrase. It names the event or process in which they gave themselves to Jesus, which changed their lives and filled them with meaning. For million of other Christians (and former Christians and non-Christians), it is primarily negative. Like *salvation* and *righteousness,* it carries a lot of baggage.

The reason for its negative associations today is that *born again* has been virtually identified with a particular way of being Christian. Polls indicate that Christians who self-identify as *born again* most often believe that:

The Bible is inerrant.

Jesus died to pay for our sins, and we can be forgiven, if we believe in him. (Google *born again* and you will find the four steps to becoming Christian, which focus on our sinfulness, Jesus dying for our sins, and the need to believe in him in order to have eternal life.)

Creation happened as narrated in Genesis, and evolution should be rejected.

Abortion is a sin, maybe even as bad as murder, and should not be legal.

Homosexuality is sinful, and the extension of equal moral and legal standing to homosexuals is wrong and to be resisted.

Christianity is "the only way" of salvation. Sometimes other religions are explicitly condemned and vilified.

Supporting a militaristic foreign policy is compatible with being Christian. Christianity's goal is going to heaven, not avoiding wars or seeking peace through justice on earth. (For example, in 2003, shortly before the American invasion of Iraq, the demographic group most in favor of going to war, indeed starting a war, was "white evangelicals" [84 percent]. Most of these, at least a strong majority, self-identify as born again.)

Not all born-again Christians affirm all of the above. But most do. To say the obvious, the phrase *born again* has become associated primarily with the Christian religious and political right, with what is often and perhaps misleadingly called "conservative Christianity." Misleadingly, because it is a stereotype, a labeling. Misleadingly, because it actually is not very conservative. A conservative is one who seeks to conserve the wisdom of the past. But much of "conservative" Christianity in our time is a modern creation, not a conservation of the riches of the Christian past.

Given the association of *born again* with this particular kind of Christianity, it is not surprising that its primary meaning is negative, even for many Christians. I have heard more than one Christian say things like, "You can be born again and still be mean," "You can be born again and still be filled with an angry righteousness in the worst sense of the word," "You can be born again and still be quite untransformed," and even, "You can be born again and still be a jerk." Their comments reflect its commonly negative meaning.

The negative associations of *born again* are unfortunate. They eclipse and obscure its rich biblical meaning. Not only rich, but important. Being *born again* is a powerful metaphor for the transformation at the center of the Christian life.

The classic New Testament *born again* passage is in John 3:1–10 (the phrase occurs only one other time in the New Testament, in 1 Pet. 1:23). It begins:

Now there was a Pharisee named Nicodemus, a leader of the Jews. He came to Jesus by night and said to him, "Rabbi, we know that you are a teacher who has come from God; for no one can do these signs that you do apart from the presence of God."

Nicodemus is identified as a Pharisee and a leader of the people. The latter means that he was among the ruling elite. He comes to Jesus "by night." In John's richly symbolic use of language, this means that he is still "in the dark." His interest in Jesus seems genuine. The text provides no reason to think that his first words to Jesus are false flattery.

Jesus answers him:

Very truly, I tell you, no one can see the kingdom of God without being born from above.

For the first time in this text, the Greek phrase often translated into English as *born again* or *born anew* appears. The translation above (the NRSV) reads "born from above." It is a better translation;

as the story later makes clear it means to be "born of the Spirit." But the difference in translations is not crucial; to be born from above is to be born anew. And in this text it is associated with the "kingdom of God."

Nicodemus asks Jesus:

> How can anyone be born after having grown old? Can one enter a second time into the mother's womb and be born?

Nicodemus takes the metaphor of being "born from above" literally and wants to know how one can possibly return to the womb. Nicodemus is a literalist; he doesn't get the symbolic meaning of this language. This happens often in John's Gospel—those "in the dark" fail to recognize the more-than-literal meaning of language.

Jesus answers:

> Very truly, I tell you, no one can enter the kingdom of God without being born of water and Spirit. What is born of the flesh is flesh, and what is born of the Spirit is spirit. Do not be astonished that I said to you, "You must be born from above." The wind blows where it chooses, and you hear the sound of it, but you do not know where it comes from or where it goes. So it is with everyone who is born of the Spirit.

Jesus emphasizes that to be born anew is to be "born of the Spirit" (three times).

Nicodemus asks him how these things can possibly be, and Jesus answers:

Are you a teacher of Israel, and yet you do not understand these things?

As the passage concludes, Nicodemus still doesn't get it, still doesn't "understand these things."

The metaphor of rebirth, being born of the Spirit, is an image of radical transformation. An old life has been left behind, and a new life has begun. It has a number of metaphorical equivalents in the New Testament. In Paul, dying and rising with Christ, being crucified with Christ, and becoming a new creation. In the synoptic Gospels, bearing the cross and following Jesus to Jerusalem, the place of death and resurrection. To be born again, to be born of the Spirit, is to die to an old identity and way of being and to be born into a new identity and way of being centered in the Spirit of God—which for Christians is known normatively in Jesus.

Thus being *born again* is utterly central to Christianity, one of the main images for the goal and promise of the Christian life. It describes our transformation and, ultimately, the transformation of the world, for those who are born of the Spirit of God as known in Jesus share God's passion for a more just and peaceful world.

# CHAPTER 17

# The Only Way

That Christianity is "the only way" of salvation has been familiar to Christians for centuries. For a long time, our Christian ancestors took it for granted. They lived in lands where everybody was Christian, or was supposed to be. They seldom if ever had contact with people of other religions. The exception was in cities where there was a Jewish population. But Jews were consistently seen as having rejected Jesus as "the only way."

This situation of Christian isolation from other religions lasted a long time. In the upper Midwest, where I grew up and went to college, I didn't know anybody who wasn't either an active or lapsed Christian. In this setting, it was easy to take it for granted that Jesus and Christianity were "the only way" of salvation.

And within the framework of heaven-and-hell Christianity, salvation meant "going to heaven." This is why we and other churches supported missionaries. In words from a familiar missionary hymn, there were souls perishing, lost in shades of night, and they needed to hear "tidings of Jesus, redemption and release."

Many Christians today continue to believe, or think that orthodox Christianity teaches that they are supposed to believe, that Jesus is the only way of salvation, the only way to heaven. It is a major element in the preaching and teaching of fundamentalist and most conservative evangelical churches. It is the reason for being Christian.

## HISTORICAL MEANING

In the first century, what did Christians mean when they proclaimed that Jesus is "the way, the truth, and the life"? Or, in words attributed to Peter in Acts 4:12: "There is salvation in no one else [other than Jesus], for there is no other name under heaven given among mortals by which we must be saved"?

These words testify to the experience of Jesus's followers. They had experienced salvation—liberation, deliverance, healing and wholeness, return from exile, light in their darkness, new creation, being born again—through Jesus. From this experience came the exclamation "He is the way!"

It is also the language of love, like the words lovers use for their beloved. When we say to our beloved, "You're the most beautiful person in the world," we are not making a factual statement that everybody should agree with. Somebody overhearing us might think, "The most beautiful person in the world? Attractive maybe—but not the most beautiful person in the world." But that would miss the point. This is the language of love, devotion, delight, commitment. This is also is part of what it means to say "Jesus is the only way."

The language is also about more than experience and love. It does make a claim. It affirms that what we see in Jesus is "the way, and the truth, and the life" and that "there is salvation in no one else." How are we to understand this claim?

One way of understanding it, probably the most common way,

is that you have to know about and believe in Jesus—that you must know about and believe in the Christian message. Note that this means that you can be saved only by knowing and believing the right language, namely, Christian language. This virtually amounts to salvation by words—by believing the right words instead of other words.

Though many American Christians believe this, many do not, because they cannot. The claim that the creator of the universe is known in only one religious tradition has become increasingly unpersuasive to many millions, in part because many of us know people of other religions and also know that all religions, including Christianity, are particular historical responses to the experience of God, the sacred, in the cultures in which they originated. How, then, can any one of them truthfully proclaim itself to be "the only way"?

There is a way of understanding the claim of John 14:6 that does not involve Christian exclusivism. The key is the realization that John is the incarnational Gospel; in it Jesus incarnates, embodies, enfleshes what can be seen of God in a human life. To say, "Jesus is the way, the truth, and the life," is to say, "What we see in Jesus is the way, the truth, and the life." It is not about knowing the word *Jesus* and believing in what is said about him that is "the way." Rather, the way is what we see in his life; we see a life of loving God and loving others, a life of challenging the powers that oppress this world, a life radically centered in the God to whom he bore witness.

In John 18:38, as Jesus appears before Pilate, the incarnational meaning of this language is clear. Pilate asks, "What is truth?" The irony is that the truth is standing before him in Jesus. What we see in Jesus is the way, the truth, and the life.

Can one know the way, the truth, and the life apart from Jesus? For me, the answer is yes. The enduring religions of the world all include lovers of God and saints in whom one can see the way, the truth, and the life. But for those of us who are Christians, we see the way, the truth, and the life preeminently in Jesus. He is our way, our truth, our life.

CHAPTER 18

# The Ascension

In the Christian liturgical year, the festival of the ascension of Jesus occurs forty days after Easter and ten days before the descent of the Holy Spirit at Pentecost. Ascension Day is observed to varying degrees in different Christian communities. I cannot recall that it was celebrated in the church of my childhood with a special service on its particular day, which was most often a weekday. We did observe it on the Sunday following Ascension Day. So we knew about it, but it was a rather minor occasion.

I was therefore surprised when I was in Germany on sabbatical in the 1980s and found out that it was a public holiday. Schools and public institutions were closed, as were most businesses. I think I was experiencing the ebbing edge of Christendom; I suspect that most European countries treated Ascension Day as a holiday, a holy day, until recently. Perhaps some still do.

Forty days as the period of time between Easter and Ascension Day is based on the story of the ascension in Acts 1:1–11. We are told that Jesus appeared to the apostles "during forty days" after his suffering. They gather together one last time in or near Jerusalem. Jesus tells them to stay in Jerusalem, where they will soon be empowered by the Holy Spirit, and commissions them to be his witnesses in the Jewish homeland and "to the ends of the earth." Then:

> When he had said this, as they were watching, he was lifted up, and a cloud took him out of their sight. While he was going and they were gazing up toward heaven, suddenly two men in white robes stood by them. They [the men in white robes] said, "Men of Galilee, why do you stand looking up toward heaven? This Jesus, who has been taken up from you into heaven, will come in the same way as you saw him go into heaven." (vv. 9–11)

Though this story in Acts doesn't specify a particular location other than Jerusalem, the ascension story in Luke (more about that soon) locates it in or near the village of Bethany on the Mount of Olives, also known as Mount Olivet, the high hill immediately to the east of Jerusalem with its dramatic vista of the Holy City. There is today, not surprisingly, a Church of the Ascension located there.

Giving this story a location is part of its visualization in the Christian imagination, beginning with Luke and continuing over the centuries. The history of Christian art is filled with visual representations of the ascension in which Jesus's followers see him going up into heaven. One famous painting shows only the feet of Jesus just under the top of the frame, the rest of him already beyond.

For many people today these visualizations along with the modern literalization of language suggest that the ascension refers to an event within the space-time world—a historical event, even if supernaturally caused, a "public" event in the sense that anybody who had been there would have seen it. Perhaps with our technology, it could have been videotaped. To use language often used in this book, this is, in harder or softer forms, a literal-factual understanding of the story.

But is this how we are to think of the ascension—as an event that either happened or didn't happen on a particular day in a particular place? Or is it about something more, something else?

The New Testament itself is very helpful here. It has two other ascension stories, neither of which mentions forty days. Strikingly, one is at the end of the Gospel of Luke, written by the same author who wrote Acts. Luke ends his Gospel with a story of Jesus ascending on the evening of Easter—not forty days later.

In Luke, the first Easter is a busy day. All of his Easter stories occur that Sunday (24:1–53). Just after dawn, the women discover the empty tomb; then Jesus walks with two of his followers on the road to Emmaus for several hours; then Jesus appears to the disciples and their companions in Jerusalem, asks for something to eat, commissions them to take the message to the "nations" (Gentiles), and commands them to remain in Jerusalem until they "have been clothed with power from on high."

Still the same day, in the final four verses of Luke, Jesus ascends into heaven:

Then Jesus led them out as far as Bethany, and, lifting up his hands, he blessed them. While he was blessing them, he withdrew from them, and was carried up into heaven. And they worshiped him, and returned to Jerusalem with great joy; and they were continually in the temple blessing God.

What are we to make of the fact that the same author tells the same story twice, but separates the two versions by forty days? One possibility is "clumsy editing"; the author forgot that he had already told the story and set it on a different day. Another possibility is that Jesus ascended twice—forty days apart. I don't imagine many take this possibility seriously. Yet another possibility is that the author is not thinking about "calendar" time, but symbolic time, metaphorical time, parabolic time—that he did not intend the story of the ascension to be understood as a particular event that happened on a particular day.

That Jesus's ascension is not to be thought of this way is suggested by what sounds like a third ascension story, even though visual imagery of Jesus "going up" is not used. In Matthew 28:16–17, his followers are in Galilee on "the mountain" to which they had been told to go. There the risen Jesus appears for the final time to his followers:

> And Jesus came and said to them: "All authority in heaven and on earth has been given to me. Go therefore and make disciples of all nations, baptizing them in the name of the Father and of the Son and of the Holy Spirit, and teaching them to obey everything that I have commanded you. And remember, I am with you always, to the end of the age." (28:18–20)

Noteworthy in this final appearance of the risen Lord in Matthew is the affirmation of authority, the command to make "disciples of all nations" (including therefore Gentiles, as in Luke and Acts) and what that means, "teaching them to obey everything that I have commanded you." It is worthwhile pausing to consider what that last phrase means—it is not about *believing* the things Jesus may have told them, but *obeying* what he commanded.

Finally, note the concluding promise. The risen Jesus says, "Remember, I am with you always." It is the promise of an abiding presence. The words echo Isaiah 7:14, which Matthew uses in his first chapter in the story of Jesus's birth. The one born to Mary will be "Emmanuel," which means "God with us." Now, as his Gospel ends, the risen Jesus says, "I am with you"—in effect, "I am Emmanuel—God with you."

As we compare this story to the stories in Luke and Acts, two things are especially striking: location and timing. Matthew's version happens in Galilee—not in or near Jerusalem, as in Luke and Acts. Indeed, in both Matthew and Mark, there are no stories of the risen Jesus appearing in Jerusalem; they happen in Galilee. And in Matthew no time period is specified, except that it would have to be long enough for the disciples to travel from Jerusalem to Galilee, a journey of at least several days.

So, are we to think of the ascension as a particular event? I think not. The way Luke (in the Gospel and Acts) and Matthew tell the story suggests not. Instead, this story has another meaning. It is a metaphorical narrative, a parabolic story, a parable about Jesus.

## METAPHORICAL MEANINGS

As a parabolic story about Jesus, its foundational meaning is that Jesus is now with God. The story makes this affirmation using the visual imagery of the three-story universe of the ancient imagination—heaven is up, hell is down, earth is in the middle. Within this framework, it portrays Jesus as ascending into heaven, the home of God. As a metaphorical narrative, its primary meaning is clear: Jesus is now with God.

This foundational meaning has a number of nuances. First,

Jesus is no longer "here"—that is, no longer here as a flesh-and-blood reality. The pre-Easter Jesus is gone. Rather, Jesus is now with God, and God is everywhere—and so Jesus is everywhere.

Second, as an immediate corollary, Jesus is no longer constrained by time and space. The historical Jesus, the pre-Easter Jesus, was—he was always in a particular place and particular time, and not "everywhere" and "every time." But now Jesus, like God, is everywhere and can be experienced, known, anytime.

Third, the ascension is associated with the lordship of Jesus, that is, with his authority. In Matthew, his final words include, "All authority in heaven and on earth has been given to me." In both of the creeds, the ascension is coupled with Jesus sitting at "the right hand of God," language rooted in the New Testament. Jesus now sits at the right hand of God.

Of course God doesn't have hands and Jesus isn't sitting somewhere, but the meaning of this language in its ancient context is clear. Whoever sat at the right hand of a king (and the imagery here is monarchical) was the most honored one, the most favored one, sometimes virtually or actually having the same authority as the king. To say that Jesus now sits at God's right hand means that Jesus is Lord, vindicated by God, raised and ascended to God's right hand.

This meaning of the ascension story raises the question embedded in so much of the New Testament and early Christianity: Who is Lord? In its first-century context, the choice was between the lordship of God, as known in Jesus, and the lordship of Caesar—by which was and is meant "this world," the humanly constructed world of domination, injustice, oppression, and violence. The lordship of Jesus means the lordship of God; it's about God's dream for the world versus the common human dreams of wealth and power that far too often have become nightmares.

Finally, the ascension story is about the abiding presence of Jesus in the experience and conviction and lives of his followers. He was for them, and still is so for Christians, "Emmanuel," to repeat language from Isaiah and Matthew, "God with us." Like the Easter stories, the ascension affirms that Jesus is not simply a figure of the past, but is present today as well. And like Easter, the ascension affirms that Jesus is Lord.

Within Luke's symbolic use of calendar time, the ascension prepares the way for the story of Pentecost ten days later. According to his ascension stories in Luke and Acts, Jesus is no longer here, but with God. But the Spirit of God, the Spirit of Christ, the Holy Spirit, is about to descend and be with his followers. The story of Pentecost is the topic of the next chapter. Ascension and Pentecost go together.

# CHAPTER 19

# Pentecost

I n the Christian liturgical calendar, Pentecost is observed ten days after Ascension Day and thus fifty days after Easter. It is one of the three most important Christian festivals, along with Christmas and Easter. It recalls and celebrates the descent of the Holy Spirit upon the followers of Jesus.

My own memories of Pentecost are vague compared to memories of Christmas and Easter. My primary recollection is that it was about the birthday of the church. In some churches, though not in mine, it was celebrated with balloons and birthday cake. My memories also associate Pentecost with the onset of summer. Except when Easter was unusually early, it was close to the end of the school year and the beginning of months of free time. On or near Pentecost, we also had our Sunday school picnic, which marked the end of Sunday school until fall. Pentecost was about summer and freedom.

Pentecost was an important Jewish festival before it became a Christian festival. One of the three pilgrimage festivals that ideally were to be spent in Jerusalem, it occurred fifty days after Passover, the commemoration of Israel's liberation from Egypt. It recalled and celebrated the giving of the covenant to Israel on Mt. Sinai.

It was about the creation of a new kind of community—a way of living together radically different from life in Egypt. This meaning and the period of fifty days were brought forward into the early Christian understanding of Pentecost.

The central affirmation of Pentecost is that the Spirit promised by Jesus is now present among his followers and in the world. The Spirit is the Spirit of God, the Holy Spirit, the Spirit of Christ. This claim is foundational to the New Testament and early Christianity.

But the *story* of the first Christian Pentecost is narrated only once, in the book of Acts. As its first chapter ends, the twelve disciples are in Jerusalem, where Jesus told them to remain until the Holy Spirit came upon them. Then at the beginning of Acts 2:

> When the day of Pentecost had come, they were all together in one place. And suddenly from heaven there came a sound like the rush of a violent wind, and it filled the entire house where they were sitting. Divided tongues, as of fire, appeared among them, and a tongue rested on each of them. All of them were filled with the Holy Spirit and began to speak in other languages, as the Spirit gave them ability.
>
> Now there were devout Jews from every nation under heaven living in Jerusalem [many of them there as pilgrims for the festival]. And at this sound the crowd gathered and was bewildered, because each heard them speaking in the native language of each. Amazed and astonished, they asked, "Are not all these who are speaking Galileans? And how is it that we hear, each of us, in our own native language? Parthians, Medes, Elamites, . . ."

The list of countries they were from continues, fifteen in all. Then, in Acts 2:11, their question becomes an exclamation: "In our own languages we hear them speaking about God's deeds of power."

Note what happens in the story. The Spirit descends as *fire* and *wind*. Both are metaphors for God's presence. In the Old Testament God speaks to Moses from a bush that burns without being consumed (Exod. 3:1–6), God is present with the Israelites in the wilderness as a pillar of fire (13:21), and God descends to Mt. Sinai in fire (19:18). And in both Hebrew and Greek, the word for *wind* is also the word for *breath* and *spirit*.

Then the emphasis turns to language. The crowd hears the disciples speaking in many languages. Perhaps because the story earlier refers to "tongues of fire," many people think of Pentecost as involving "speaking in tongues" ( *glossolalia*) in the sense that Paul refers to it at the beginning of 1 Corinthians 14. There, as one of the gifts of the Spirit, it is an unintelligible prayer language. In some Christian churches today, usually called "charismatic" churches, speaking in tongues in this sense is considered an indication that one has been filled with the Spirit.

But in the story of Pentecost, this is not what is meant. Instead, the descent of the Spirit as "tongues of fire" enables the disciples to speak in a universally understood language. The individuals in the crowd, from multiple countries with diverse languages, all hear the disciples speaking in *their own* language, as they twice exclaim.

The metaphorical meaning of this part of the story is illuminated by the way it makes use of a well-known story in the Old Testament, the Tower of Babel in Genesis 11. The story is strategically located between two portions of the Genesis narrative. The first portion is the "prehistory" of Israel, which includes the creation stories, Eden, the primordial ancestors, Noah and the flood, and a new beginning. Then comes the story of the Tower of Babel, whose conclusion is the scattering of the nations into different language groups, so that they are no longer one. It is followed in Genesis 12 by the beginning of the patriarchal narratives, God's call of Abraham and covenant with Abraham.

To briefly review the story in Genesis 11, it begins, "Now the whole earth had one language and the same words." The people then build a city and "a tower with its top in the heavens." In vividly anthropomorphic language—language that personifies God—we are told, "The Lord came down to see the city and the tower." Then God decides to scatter the people over the earth, giving them different languages. The reason for God's judgment? "This [the building of the city and the tower] is only the beginning of what they will do." The story ends with the people scattered over the earth, no longer able to understand one another. The narrator concludes, "Therefore it was called Babel, because there the Lord confused the language of all the earth." In Hebrew, there is a wordplay between the word *Babel* and the word *confused*. In English, the word *babble* comes from this story. Babble is language we don't understand.

The echoing of Babel in Luke's story of Pentecost has a powerful metaphorical meaning. Pentecost is the reversal of Babel. What happened at Babel confused the world by dividing it into separate languages and countries, resulting in misunderstanding, rivalries, and conflict. Pentecost is the beginning of the reunification of humanity.

The echo of Babel should not distract from the foundational meaning of Pentecost. It concerns the descent of the Spirit promised by Jesus and thus the continuation of his presence and the movement he had begun.

In the New Testament as a whole, the Spirit of God, the Holy Spirit, the Spirit of the risen Christ is central. In the rest of Acts, the Spirit is the main character. The two primary human characters are Peter and Paul—but they are guided by the Spirit, as are other early Christians in Acts.

Paul not only speaks about the "gifts of the Spirit" (the greatest of which is love, according to 1 Cor. 13), but also about life "in the Spirit." He uses the phrase many times and as a synonym for life "in Christ," which he uses even more often. In one of his more magnificent passages, he identifies the Spirit and Christ, the risen Jesus:

> Now the Lord is the Spirit, and where the Spirit of the
> Lord is, there is freedom. And all of us, with unveiled faces,
> seeing the glory of the Lord as though reflected in a mirror,
> are being transformed into the same image [the image or
> likeness of Christ] from one degree of glory to another; for
> this comes from the Lord, the Spirit. (2 Cor. 3:17–18)

Note that the Lord, the risen Christ, is the Spirit.

So also in John's Gospel. The risen Jesus bestows the Holy Spirit on his followers on the night of Easter (and not fifty days later, suggesting again that we are not dealing with calendar time): "He breathed on them and said to them, 'Receive the Holy Spirit'" (20:22). It is the fulfillment of the promise of Jesus in John 14:15–31, part of his farewell discourse in John 13–17. God will give them "the Spirit of truth"; Jesus will not leave them orphaned, but will come to them; God will send the Holy Spirit in Jesus's name. In John, the coming of the Spirit is the return of Jesus. In John 3, the famous "born again" passage means to be born "from above," that is, from the Spirit.

Thus Pentecost is about the abiding presence of Jesus as the Holy Spirit. In Luke's Gospel, the public activity of Jesus begins with the descent of the Spirit upon him: "The Spirit of the Lord is upon me" (4:18). From the cross, Jesus's final words are, "Father, into your hands I commend my spirit" (23:46). The spirit that was in Jesus returns to God and then is given to the community at Pentecost.

In the Christian calendar, the Sunday after Pentecost is Trinity Sunday. The progression, the sequence, is metaphorically and symbolically perfect. Advent, Christmas, Epiphany, Lent, Holy Week, and Easter have been about God and God's incarnation in Jesus. Now, with the descent of the Holy Spirit on Pentecost, the Trinity is complete—and so we celebrate it on Trinity Sunday.

# CHAPTER 20

# The Rapture and the Second Coming

Most Christians throughout history and also today have never heard of the *rapture*. With good reason. The word and the notion it embodies are a modern innovation, going back less than two centuries. Nobody had thought of it until the 1800s. But for millions of American Christians today, mostly conservative Protestants, the *rapture* is an essential part of their faith and understanding of what it means to be Christian.

For these Christians, the rapture begins the scenario that will unfold seven years before the second coming of Jesus and the final judgment. More specifically, it refers to an event when true Christians will be *raptured,* that is, taken up to heaven, before Jesus's second coming. Those who are raptured will be spared the "tribulation"—the horrific suffering, wars, and devastation that face those who are "left behind."

The rapture is the premise of the appropriately named "Left Behind" novels that have sold more than sixty million copies since they began to be published in the mid-1990s. All twelve in the original series have been on the *New York Times* bestselling fiction list. Note: the fiction list, praise the Lord.

The novels are about what happens to those left behind after the rapture occurs. In the seven years before the final judgment, they still have a chance to repent by committing themselves to Jesus. Many of those who repent become part of a "tribulation force" that battles with military weapons the forces of the Antichrist—who not surprisingly is the head of the United Nations. As the armies clash at the battle of Armageddon, Jesus returns to earth and destroys the armies of the Antichrist, and then the final judgment occurs. Jesus is not only an omnipotent warrior, but also condemns most people to eternal suffering in hell.

How many of the millions of readers of these books take their vision of Christianity seriously? It's hard to know—but I suspect most do. I doubt that the novels had many readers beyond those who were at least open to the premise that the rapture will happen someday, and it could be soon.[1]

The "Left Behind" novels have ancestry. In the 1970s, the rapture was the main theme in the bestselling books by Hal Lindsey, including *The Late Great Planet Earth*. The rapture and the signs that it and the second coming may be soon are the theme of "prophecy conferences" in fundamentalist and conservative churches.

Believing in the rapture and believing that Jesus is coming *soon* are not the same thing. You can believe in the latter but not the former, as has happened from time to time in Christian history. There have been periods when many Christians thought the second coming was at hand—in early Christianity, again as the year 1000 drew near, again during the Reformation of the 1500s. There have also been small Christian groups throughout history who have thought Jesus was coming soon, such as the Millerites in upstate New York in the 1840s. But none of these expectations of Jesus's imminent return included the rapture.

Yet in contemporary American Christianity, the two typically do go together. Most who believe in the rapture also think it could be soon, and most who believe that the second coming of Jesus may be soon also believe in the rapture. One poll I am aware of reports that about 20 percent of American Christians are "certain" that the second coming will happen in the next fifty years, and another 20 percent think it "likely." My hunch is that most who believe that the second coming is soon also believe in the rapture. They belong to churches that teach the rapture and the imminent return of Jesus.

## THE RAPTURE IN HISTORICAL PERSPECTIVE

Because millions of Christians think that the rapture is "biblical teaching" and thus has the authority of the Bible behind it, it is important to know that it is neither biblical nor ancient, but was first proclaimed by a British evangelist named John Nelson Darby (1800–82). He found it in his interpretation of a few passages in the Bible that speak about the second coming of Jesus and the end of the world, especially in one of Paul's letters, 1 Thessalonians:

> For the Lord himself, . . . will descend from heaven, and the dead in Christ will rise first. Then we who are alive, who are left, will be caught up in the clouds together with them to meet the Lord in the air; and so we will be with the Lord forever. (4:16–17)

However this text is interpreted, the important point is that no Christian interpreter had ever seen the rapture in this text until Darby. The rapture is a modern invention.

Though Darby was British, he had more impact in America than in England. Part of his legacy is the *Scofield Reference Bible,* the first edition of which was published in 1909. In its footnotes, it divides world history into multiple dispensations climaxing in the rapture and the second coming of Jesus. The *Scofield Bible* has shaped what many American Protestants think the Bible and Christianity are about.

Knowing that the rapture is a modern invention matters for more than one reason. Christians who have never heard of it and wonder if they've overlooked something of importance need not worry. It is not biblical, not ancient or traditional Christian teaching.

The other reason it is important is that millions of American Christians believe in it and expect that it and the second coming might be soon. This belief seriously distorts what Christianity and the Christian life are about. Note what happens when the rapture and the imminent return of Jesus are emphasized:

> This world doesn't matter very much—what matters is being ready for the rapture and the judgment. If everything might end in the next fifty years, why work to improve political and economic structures? They're all going to end soon. How much does the environment matter? It doesn't have to last much longer. And peace? Rapture theology portrays the end times as marked by wars and rumors of wars. Working for peace might actually get in the way of the rapture and the second coming. At the very least, it is an illusion to think there can peace on earth.

Rapture theology and the "Left Behind" novels are filled with violence—not just the violence of the forces of the Antichrist, but divine violence. God and Jesus are violent, involved in the destruction of the world and evildoers. Jesus's followers are violent; they war against the Antichrist. The climax of history is a great battle—Armageddon. What kind of theology are you likely to have if you think of God and Jesus as violent?

Rapture theology is also self-interested. It is all about being "right with God" when the rapture occurs, so that you will be taken up to heaven to escape the suffering of the world. Is this what Christianity is about?

There will be no rapture. Christianity's goal is not escape from this world. It loves this world and seeks to change it for the better.

## The Second Coming

Apart from rapture theology, will there be a second coming of Jesus? Will Jesus someday come again on a date in calendrical time, whether that is soon or centuries, millennia, or millions of years in the future?

Probably most Christians believe (or think they are supposed to believe) that Jesus will come again. Passages in the New Testament refer to Jesus coming again. It is affirmed in the creeds commonly recited in Christian worship. Jesus "will come again to judge the living and the dead."

So, will Jesus come again? It depends upon what we imagine that phrase to mean. One way of imagining it is as a future event that will be seen and experienced by everybody who is alive when it happens—as the kind of event that could in principle be video-taped. But it might not make the cable news networks, because "it would all be over" before they could broadcast it. Is this what the second coming is—an event that some people someday in the future will experience?

A number of verses in the New Testament—in the Gospels, Paul's letters, and Revelation—speak of the second coming of Jesus as *soon,* in the writers' generation or at least while some of their generation were still alive. If we take this language liter-ally, it means they were wrong—it didn't happen *soon* from their point in time. One way of dealing with this is to say that they were right about the expectation (there will be a second coming of Jesus someday in which he will judge the living and the dead), but wrong about thinking that *soon* meant in their time. This under-standing—that Jesus will come again someday—is part of heaven-and-hell Christianity. Perhaps it will happen soon or maybe not for a long time. But being Christian means believing in the second coming—that it will happen.

It is difficult to imagine what it means to affirm that the second coming of Jesus will occur on a future date as an event in space and time. If Jesus literally (even if supernaturally) comes back to earth on a particular day, will he come to a particular place? Perhaps Jerusalem? Or, as a contemporary joke asks, to Rome or Salt Lake City? Or do we imagine that he will come again everywhere at the same time? If so, can one imagine a "figure" doing this? A flash of light that encompasses the whole earth, perhaps—but a "person"?

The point is that when we try to imagine the second coming of Jesus as something that will happen someday in the space-time world, it vanishes. Can you imagine such an event when you think about it? I cannot. And I do not think this is because of our limited imagination.

So, what did it mean when first-century Christians affirmed that Jesus would come again? It was an expression of their conviction that what had begun in Jesus would be completed and come to fruition. Jesus was not just the past and the present, but also the future; his passion was the coming of the kingdom of God, the dream of God, for the earth.

Some of his followers in the first century were convinced that it would happen soon. In that, they were obviously wrong. It didn't happen. But were they wrong in their passion for the vision of the world they saw embodied in Jesus and their conviction that this was the future? To affirm that Jesus will come again to complete what he began is to make a commitment to his vision of the future, the dream of God.

So, will there be a second coming on some day in the future? I think not. Its meaning is not literal-factual. Rather, the affirmation of the second coming has more-than-literal meanings. It is the return of Jesus already experienced as the risen Christ and the Spirit of Christ. It is Jesus coming again in the rhythms of the Christian liturgical year. Advent is preparing for the coming of Jesus—about the coming again of the Christ who is already here. Jesus also comes again in the Eucharist; in the bread and wine Christ becomes present to us. And what is meant by the second coming is also the ultimate Christian hope—for that time, to use Paul's language, when "God [will] be all in all" (1 Cor. 15:28).

# CHAPTER 21

# Heaven

*H*eaven in common Christian usage is most often associated with a blessed afterlife. Its opposite is hell. For most Christians, there is also a third option, purgatory. Purgatory is a place of purification after death for those who are neither saintly enough to go immediately to heaven nor so irredeemably evil that they must go to hell.

In the Bible, *heaven* has a number of meanings that are not about an afterlife. Sometimes the word means the abode of God, as in the opening line of the Lord's Prayer, "Our Father in heaven." Sometimes the word simply means the sky, as in the magnificent vision that begins in Revelation 21:1: "Then I saw a new heaven and a new earth"—that is, a new sky and a new earth.

Sometimes it is a synonym for *God,* as often in Matthew's Gospel. Where Mark and Luke use the phrase the "kingdom of God," Matthew uses the phrase the "kingdom of heaven" (actually plural in Greek, so that it should be translated "kingdom of *the heavens*"). With this phrase, Matthew means the "kingdom of God" and knows that it is for the earth. His version of the Lord's Prayer includes "Your kingdom come . . . *on earth* as it is in heaven." But he uses "kingdom of heaven" ("the heavens"), because of his Jewish reverential avoidance of the word *God*.

But none of these uses is relevant to the common identification of *heaven* with a blessed afterlife.

Yet heaven as the hope for life beyond physical death has been part of Christianity for a long time. It was there, but had not yet come to the forefront in the early centuries of Christianity, and may not have done so until around 1000.[1] But since then, the afterlife has been so central that it has been the primary motive (along with the threat of hell) for being Christian.

So what might we think about an afterlife? I state my personal view. Of course, the whole of this book is my personal view. All any writer, ancient or contemporary, can do is to say, "This is how I see things." None of us can escape our personal vantage point. But in this book I have sought to report how mainstream biblical and theological scholars (meaning those not committed to biblical inerrancy and literalism) see things. Now I share how I think of the afterlife without knowing how widely my view would be affirmed by mainstream Christian scholars.

In the precise sense of the word, I am an agnostic about what happens after death. An *agnostic* is "one who doesn't know." Agnosticism is not a halfway house between believing and atheism. It is a state of "not knowing." I do not know what happens after death—and I am aware that I cannot resolve my uncertainty by deciding to believe something in particular. Believing does not make something true. For example, I could decide to believe that the earth and the universe were created no more than ten thousand years ago. But believing that has nothing to do with whether it's true.

Among the things I do not know: I do not know that there is no afterlife. Indeed, I find research on near-death experiences intriguing. Some of what is consistently reported as part of these experiences suggests that we do enter another realm at death, for example, the tunnel, the bright light, the experience of leaving the body and seeing things from a vantage point outside the body. Who knows what this means?

And if there is a blessed afterlife, there is much that seems impossible to know. For example, if there is life beyond death, is it about heaven or hell—and maybe even purgatory? Most Christians have believed in purgatory—only Protestants reject it.

Or is an afterlife about reincarnation? Though we commonly think of reincarnation in connection with Buddhism and Hinduism, a significant minority of Christians have affirmed it from antiquity to the present. Some early Christian theologians, such as Origen around 200, believed in reincarnation. Not until the end of the 500s was it declared heretical by Pope Gregory the Great. He wouldn't have had to do so unless some Christians affirmed it. I was surprised by polls indicating that about one-fourth of American Catholics today and about 20 percent of American Protestants believe in reincarnation. So, heaven, hell, and purgatory—or reincarnation?

If there is a blessed afterlife, and I'm there, will I know that I am me? That is, is personal identity preserved in an afterlife? For some people, this seems like a ludicrous question. If the afterlife isn't about you and I knowing that we are you and I, what's it about? Yet when I think of my best experiences in this life, they have been those in which I was so completely caught up in what I was experiencing that there was no part of me left over that was aware that "I'm Marcus and I'm having this experience." If the best experiences of our lives are moments when we are not conscious of being this particular self, would an afterlife in which we know that we're a particular self be an inferior state of affairs?

The next question is a variation of the previous one. If there is a blessed afterlife, are there family reunions? If so, is this good or bad news? For some people, family has been the greatest source of joy in their lives, and the prospect of being reunited with those they love is immensely attractive. But for others, family has been one of the greatest sources of pain and suffering. Does an afterlife mean that we will be with these people forever? Do the relationships we have now continue?

Puzzlement about this is the premise of the question asked of Jesus by the Sadducees in Mark 12:18–27. If a woman has been married to seven different men, whose wife will she be in the hereafter? Jesus's answer suggests radical discontinuity between this life and the next: "When they rise from the dead, they neither marry nor are given in marriage, but are like angels in heaven." What does that mean? Finally, the passage ends with another puzzling statement from Jesus: God "is God not of the dead, but of the living; you are quite wrong." God is not God of the dead, but of the living? What does that mean? Perhaps the whole is a nonanswer to the Sadducees question. Or if taken as an answer, it suggests at the very least that the afterlife is very different from a continuation of the relationships we have in this life.

So also there is ambiguity about the degree of continuity in what Paul says about resurrection in 1 Corinthians 15:35–50. There he contrasts two kinds of bodies, translated as "a physical body" and "a spiritual body." He uses an image that speaks of both continuity and discontinuity between the two. The physical body is like a seed, the spiritual body is like the full-grown plant. Continuity? Yes. The seed becomes the plant. But think of how different the full-grown plant is from the seed.

Finally, if there is a blessed afterlife, I cannot imagine that it is only for Christians. To imagine that the creator of the universe has chosen to be adequately known in only one religious tradition, which just happens to be our own, is, for me, beyond belief.

For these reasons, I am an agnostic about what happens after death. I do not even know what I would prefer—not that my preferences have anything to do with what will be. What I am convinced of is this. When we die, we do not die into nothingness, but we die into God. For me, that is enough. I can affirm with Paul in Romans:

> We do not live to ourselves, and we do not die to ourselves.
> If we live, we live to the Lord, and if we die, we die to the
> Lord; so then, whether we live or whether we die, we are
> the Lord's. (14:7–8)

I am fond of two statements attributed to Martin Luther, the mentor of my youth. I cannot quote them directly, but I am confident of the "gist." In one, he said that the afterlife is God's business, and so he didn't have to worry about it. In the other, he said that we can know as little about life after death as a baby traveling down the birth canal can know about the world the baby is about to enter.

So, is there an afterlife, and if so, what will it be like? I don't have a clue. But I am confident that the one who has buoyed us up in life will also buoy us up through death. We die into God. What more that means, I do not know. But that is all I need to know.

# CHAPTER 22

# The Creeds and the Trinity

In Catholic, Orthodox, and many mainline Protestant churches, reciting a creed—an affirmation of faith that begins with "I believe" or "we believe," followed by a series of statements about God, Jesus, and the Holy Spirit—is part of every worship service.

Western Christians use two creeds, the Apostles' Creed and the Nicene Creed; Eastern Orthodox Christians use only the latter. Both creeds have three sections, called *articles*. All of them are about God. The first article is about God as creator, the second about God as known in Jesus, and the third about God as the Holy Spirit. Thus the creeds have a trinitarian pattern, even though the word *Trinity* does not appear in them. So we will also treat the Trinity near the end of this chapter.

For many Christians, the creeds have become a problem. If I were to make a list of the ten questions I am most frequently asked, high on that list would be, "What are we going to do with the creeds?" The question is usually followed by, "I can't say them anymore." The reason is that many Christians are uncomfortable professing affirmation of a list of statements they think they are supposed to believe to be literally and absolutely true.

I focus on the Nicene Creed, in part for the sake of economy of exposition; to treat both would make this chapter too long. Beyond that, the issues for contemporary Christians raised by the Nicene Creed are very much the same as the issues raised by the Apostles' Creed. When I use *creed* in the singular, I mean the Nicene Creed.

My purpose is not to provide a line-by-line commentary. That would require book-length exposition, and there are a number of books that do that well.[1] Rather, my purpose is to address the problems that many have with the creed, especially its use of the word *believe* and the notion that the language of the creed is to be understood literally and absolutely. As I do so, I use the historical-metaphorical approach to Christian language that we have used throughout this book.

## THE NICENE CREED

The Nicene Creed is mostly about Jesus. Though it has three articles, the first about God as creator is brief—only a sentence long. So is the third article about the Holy Spirit. In the initial formulation of the creed in 325, it is only one sentence long. The fuller exposition of the third article about the Holy Spirit was added in 381 at the Council of Constantinople,

Although most readers of this book are familiar with the Nicene Creed, some may not be, and some may need reminding of what it says. As you read it, note how much of it is about Jesus.[2]

*Article One.* We believe in one God, the Father, the Almighty, maker of heaven and earth, of all that is, seen and unseen.

*Article Two.* We believe in one Lord, Jesus Christ, the only Son of God, eternally begotten of the Father, God from God, Light from Light, true God from true God, begotten, not made, of one Being with the Father.

Through him all things were made. For us and for our salvation he came down from heaven: by the power of the Holy Spirit he became incarnate from the Virgin Mary, and was made man. For our sake he was crucified under Pontius Pilate; he suffered death and was buried. On the third day he rose again in accordance with the Scriptures; he ascended into heaven and is seated at the right hand of the Father. He will come again in glory to judge the living and the dead, and his kingdom will have no end.

*Article Three* (as mentioned, the Nicene Creed of 325 ended with a single sentence about the Holy Spirit. The fuller ending was added in 381). We believe in the Holy Spirit, the Lord, the giver of Life, who proceeds from the Father and the Son. With the Father and the Son he is worshipped and glorified. He has spoken through the Prophets. We believe in one holy catholic and apostolic Church. We acknowledge one baptism for the forgiveness of sins. We look for the resurrection of the dead, and the life of the world to come. Amen.

Some critics of the creed today emphasize that even though it is mostly about Jesus, it says nothing about the historical life of Jesus—his message, teaching, and public activity. It moves from his birth to his death with nothing in between. To the extent that this implies that his teaching and activity do not matter very much, it is a valid criticism. But this was not the purpose of the Nicene Creed.

Illumination about how to understand the Nicene Creed is provided by placing it in its historical setting. The Council of Nicea was convened in 325 CE by Constantine, the first "Christian" ruler of the Roman Empire. In 313, he had legalized Christianity, thereby bringing imperial persecution of Christians to an end.

His passion was the unification of the empire. He had accomplished this militarily and politically by defeating his rival, Maxentius, in 312. Religiously, he hoped to unify the empire through Christianity. But in the years since his legalization of Christianity, he became aware that Christians were deeply divided theologically about the "nature" of Jesus.

To resolve the conflict, he called the bishops of the church together at his palace on the shore of Lake Nicea in Asia Minor, not far from today's Istanbul. The bishops—some maimed and blinded from Roman persecutions that had ended not very long ago—were treated royally. They were provided with imperial transportation to Nicea and imperial hospitality, accommodation, and banquets after they arrived.

Constantine's agenda was to reach agreement about the nature of Jesus, so that conflicts within Christianity would not lead to conflicts within his empire. He seems not to have cared what the bishops concluded—only that they came to an agreement.

For the bishops, the issue was the relationship of Jesus to God. Both sides agreed that Jesus was divine. But was he one with God—"of one substance" with God, "of one Being" with God ("of one substance," "of one Being" are alternative English translations)? Or was he a little bit less than God; divine, yes, but created by God and thus not equal with God? The first position was represented by Athanasius (293–373), the second by Arius (ca. 250–336). Athanasius won.

The difference between Arius's and Athanasius's positions matters greatly to Christians today who are concerned with what they regard as doctrinal orthodoxy. To others, the difference either is unknown or seems a bit obscure, if not arcane.

The difference it made in the fourth century was considerable. It provoked heated and sometimes violent controversy among Christians. Moreover, an issue was at stake that Constantine seemed initially not to understand (recall that his interest was not the particular result, but agreement). Like Roman emperors before him, Constantine was hailed as divine, Son of God, and Lord.

But he was not, to use the language of the creed, "begotten and not made." He was not "of one substance," "one Being" with God. Athanasius's interpretation put Jesus above the emperor. Whether Arius's interpretation made Jesus and the emperor equal is less clear. But emphatically, the Nicene Creed made the status of Jesus as divine and Son of God higher than the status of the emperor. Within a few years of Nicea, Constantine realized this and became "Arian," that is, an advocate of the lesser status of Jesus advocated by Arius. So did his imperial successors for much of the fourth century.

Thus a major issue at stake in the Nicene Creed is: Is Jesus above all of the lords of this world or is he one among a number of lords? The issue continues to come up for Christians today. Is Jesus above the lords of culture or is he one allegiance among a number of allegiances? Are we to give our allegiance to Jesus in the religious realm and our allegiance to others in the other realms of life? Are our religious and political loyalties separate? Or is

Jesus lord of all lords? The answer of the Nicene Creed (and the New Testament before it) is clear. Jesus as Lord and Son of God transcends all other lords.

Given this, standing and saying the Nicene Creed is a subversive act. Its affirmations negate the claims of other lords upon us. God as known in Jesus is Lord, the one and only Lord. The lords of culture—and they are many—are not.

Setting the Nicene Creed in its historical context has another implication. As a fourth-century product, it uses the language of our religious ancestors in that century. It, like everything expressed in words, is a historically conditioned and historically relative product.

Some of its most important language is drawn from Greek philosophy—such as *substance* or *Being* and the distinction between *begotten* and *created* (or *made*). Some of its language, especially its summation of Jesus, is drawn from the New Testament. If the most important Christian creed had been written in a different time and place, it would not have used the language of *substance* or *Being* and its summary of what matters most about Jesus might have been quite different. It may not have spoken of Jesus as God's *only* son. I became vividly aware of this when I was in South Africa in the 1990s. I was told by a group of black South African Christians that an *only son* was not as high a status as *eldest brother*. The reason was that an *only son* was a social isolate, whereas *eldest brother* was somebody you did have access to.

Moreover, the notion that the language of the creed is to be understood literally and absolutely is strange when you think about it. Jesus "came down from heaven" and later "ascended into heaven." Is heaven up? "He is seated at the right hand of the Father." Does God have hands, and is God a father, a male being? Is this language to be taken seriously? Yes. Is it to be taken literally? No.

I love the memory that Kathleen Norris shares in one of her books about the Presbyterian congregation she was part of in a small town in South Dakota. When they stood to say the creed— "God from God, Light from Light, true God from true God, begotten not made . . ."— she was struck by how much the language reminded her of the poetry of William Blake. The creed's language is the language of poetry, mystical poetry, not the language of literal factuality. Does Jesus matter greatly and decisively for Christians? Yes. Is our language about him to be understood literally? No.

As mentioned above and as Christians know, the creed begins with "I believe" or "we believe." For modern Christians who have problems with the creed, the issue is the common contemporary meaning of the word *believe*. Recall Chapter 10, where we noted that the modern meaning of the word is affirming statements to be true, most often statements that are not transparently credible. Recall also that the premodern Christian meaning of *believe* is *belove,* to give one's love, allegiance, and commitment not to a set of statements, but to somebody. "I believe" means "I give my heart to."

This realization significantly changes our understanding of what we are doing when we say the creed. Imagine substituting the word *belove* for *believe*. "I belove God," I give my heart to God. And who is that? The "maker of heaven and earth, of all that is seen and unseen," and who is known decisively in Jesus. "I belove Jesus." And who is that? The one in whom we see the decisive revelation of God. "I belove the Holy Spirit." And who is that? "The Lord, the giver of life," "who has spoken through the Prophets," and who is the continuing presence of God as known in Jesus. Believing as beloving is not believing in the literal and absolute truth of statements. It is beloving God as known in Jesus and the Spirit.

## The Creed and Christian Community

All of the above is helpful for Christians who struggle with or puzzle about the creed. In addition, consider another fact. Many organizations perform rituals that reaffirm group identity when they gather. For example, I have been told that at meetings of one of the fraternal organizations (The Elks? The Moose?), members stand and recite a set of words as they make their hands into antlers by placing their outspread fingers to the sides of their heads. This is one of the things they do when they get together. It means they belong to the community that does this.

I do not mean that saying the creed is exactly like making your hands into antlers. But saying the creed is identifying with the community that says these words together. The identification transcends space and time. It is global. Christians all around the world, in a multitude of languages, are joined together by these words. The identification transcends time as well; present and past are joined. When we say the creed, we identify with Christians who have said or heard these words for over fifteen hundred years. It is a momentary participation in the communion of saints, living and dead.

Not all churches today use the creed. Fundamentalist and evangelical churches generally do not. Some progressive or liberal Protestant congregations no longer do so. But many Christians belong to churches that regularly do. Their "official" liturgies include the creed.

For these churches, the issue is how to deal with the problems many people have with the creed. Part of the solution is education about the creed, such as suggested in this chapter. But many church members have not been exposed to such education. Moreover, I have been told that visitors or newcomers to Christian worship are often put off by the creed. "This is all new to me and I am supposed to stand and say I believe all these things? Is this what it means to be a Christian?"

So how do we "signal" both to regular members and visitors that the creed is not a set of absolutely and literally true statements that are to be believed, in the modern sense of that word? Two suggestions.

First, the creed can be sung. My own denomination's hymn book provides musical settings for the creed. The reason this can be helpful is that people seldom think that the language of song is to be taken literally. For example, millions of Christians have sung the great missionary hymn that begins, "Jesus shall reign where'er the sun does its successive journeys run." Taken literally, the words imply that the sun goes around the earth. But I have never heard a Christian say, "I can't sing that hymn anymore."

The point is not that the words of something we sing do not matter. They matter very much, in part because things we sing often lodge in our memory more strongly than things we say. Consider how many lines from songs, secular and sacred, you can recall. Moreover, the words we sing matter, because they can be vapid or powerful. But the issue of literalism doesn't arise.

Second, some liturgical congregations have begun to use a number of creeds rather than simply the two ancient ones. I am aware of two forms this takes. In one, the Nicene Creed is used every other Sunday, and a variety of contemporary creeds are used on the Sundays in between. In the other, the Nicene Creed is used once a month and other creeds on the rest of the Sundays. The effect is the same. Using a variety of creeds makes the point that there is more than one way of saying what it is we believe—

or better, who it is we belove. No particular creed, not even the Nicene Creed, is absolute. They are all historical products that use the language of their time and place. Do affirmations of faith matter? Yes. Is there only one way of making that affirmation? No. There are only historically and culturally conditioned ways of doing so.

## THE TRINITY

The Christian doctrine of the Trinity affirms, in shorthand, "one God in three persons." Like the Nicene Creed, the doctrine of the Trinity is a fourth-century product. And just as the Nicene Creed is a problem for many contemporary Christians, so also is the Trinity.

A major reason for this is the word *person* and its common meaning in modern English. It suggests a distinct center of personality and thus a distinct being. When *person* is understood this way, the Trinity seems to affirm that God is like a committee of three people, God the creator, God the Son, and God the Spirit.

Thus it is not surprising that many Jews and Muslims, Christianity's closest relatives, understand the Trinity to be an abandonment of monotheism and an affirmation of "tri-theism." But this understanding of the Trinity, whether by Christians or Jews and Muslims, is not the ancient meaning of the Trinity.

The language used in the Trinity (though not yet the doctrine) goes back to the New Testament. In the 50s, Paul's blessing at the end of one of his letters refers to God, Jesus, and the Holy Spirit: "The grace of the Lord Jesus Christ, the love of God, and the communion of the Holy Spirit be with all of you" (2 Cor. 13:13). In Matthew's Gospel, written around 90, the risen Christ commands his followers to "make disciples of all nations, baptizing them in name of the Father, and of the Son, and of the Holy Spirit" (28:19).

But the doctrine of the Trinity—meaning an officially formulated teaching—took time to develop. Implicit in the three articles of the creed, it became explicit later in the fourth century, especially in the brilliantly poetic theology of Basil of Caesarea, Gregory of Nyssa, and Gregory Naziansus, known together as the Cappadocian fathers, named after the area in central Asia Minor (now Turkey) where they lived.

Why do Christians affirm a *threefoldness* to God? Many religions affirm a *twofoldness* to God, implicitly or explicitly. Even Christianity's monotheistic relatives Judaism and Islam do. For both, God is transcendent and immanent, more than everything and yet present throughout the universe. Hinduism also affirms a twofoldness to ultimate reality, fully transcendent as *brahman* and immanent within each of us as *atman*. Religions, including monotheistic religions, are typically *binitarian,* to use a word that is not a word.

The question is why Christians add a third to this twofold affirmation about God. The answer is obvious—because of Jesus. The reason that Christianity moved from the twofold monotheism of Judaism to a threefold monotheism is because of the significance of Jesus for his followers in the first century and continuing in the centuries since then. He was for them the decisive revelation of God—and continues to be that for Christians. This is what makes somebody Christian: seeing the decisive, normative revelation, disclosure, epiphany of God in Jesus. The Trinity is thus a testimony, witness, tribute to the centrality of Jesus for Christians.

In both Greek and Latin, the meaning of the word translated into English as *person* is quite different from its modern meaning. In the fourth century when trinitarian doctrine was formulated, the word *persona* in Latin and its Greek equivalent *prosopon* referred to the mask worn by actors in the theater. Actors wore masks not for the sake of concealment (as we might wear Halloween masks today), but to play different roles. The etymology of the Latin *persona* reflects this; its roots mean "to speak through," "to sound through." In a quite literal sense, *persona* as a mask is something an actor speaks through. Applied to the Trinity, the ancient meaning of *persona/prosopon* suggests that for Christians the one God is known and speaks in three primary roles or ways: as creator and the God of Israel; in Jesus; and through the Spirit.

The above is sometimes called an *external* understanding of the Trinity, because it concerns three primary modes of revelation, three primary roles in which we experience and know God. Some theologians have argued that the Trinity is also about *internal* relations *within* God (or within the *Godhead,* a term often used for the unity that underlies the Trinity).

In a general way, the suggestion that there are internal relationships within God makes an important claim. It produces a relational model of God and thus a relational model of reality. Reality is not static, but dynamic and relational. But when theological disputes break out about what those internal relationships are like, I wonder whether we are trying to know too much.

The most famous of those disputes is the one that caused the Great Schism within Christianity in the eleventh century. The issue was whether the Holy Spirit "proceeds" from "the Father" or from "the Father and the Son." The Western church affirmed the latter, and the Eastern church the former. In 1054, Christianity split in two over this issue, producing Roman Catholicism and Eastern Orthodoxy. Each side excommunicated the other.

There is something at stake in this issue, even as it's unclear that the two sides in the conflict had any inkling of it. And that is if God's Spirit "proceeds" from "the Father and the Son" (and not from "the Father only"), then God can be known only through Jesus and thus only in Christianity. But if God's Spirit "proceeds" from "the Father only," then it is possible that God can be known apart from Jesus and thus in other religions.

To return to the main point, speaking confidently about the nature of *internal* relationships between the three persons of the Trinity is problematic. How could we ever know? But when we focus on the *external* meaning of the Trinity, its claim is clear. God is one (Christians are monotheists), and God is known to us in three primary ways.

# CHAPTER 23

# The Lord's Supper

G athering at a table for bread and wine has been an essential practice in Christianity from its beginning and continues to be celebrated as the primary Christian sacrament. For Protestants, there are only two sacraments; the other one is baptism, a once-in-a-lifetime event. Thus this meal of bread and wine is the only sacrament that Protestants experience again and again. Although Catholics have seven sacraments, the Mass is the most important and most frequently observed sacrament.

So what does this sacrament of bread and wine mean? I begin with my memories, even though they may not be typical. In the church of my childhood, Communion (as we called it) happened infrequently—once a quarter and thus four times a year. But I'm not sure about the summer—so maybe it happened only three times a year. We were quite sure that doing it more often cheapened it by making it nothing special. Besides, doing it every Sunday was what Catholics did, and we weren't Catholic.

Our Communion liturgy emphasized "worthiness"—being worthy to receive the bread and wine as the body and blood of Christ. The proof text was 1 Corinthians 11:27–29. Taking worthiness seriously meant that it was important not to go forward for Communion every time it was offered. If you did, it meant that you thought you were worthy—and that created comment and suspicion: "Look who thinks they're worthy."

Substitutionary sacrifice was also clearly involved in our use of bread and wine as the body and blood of Jesus. Our Communion liturgy was filled with images of sin, guilt, and Jesus as the sacrifice for our sins. This understanding is still embedded in many eucharistic liturgies today.

Disagreements about how the bread and wine are the body and blood of Jesus have divided Western Christians since the Protestant Reformation five hundred years ago. Catholics believe in *transubstantiation,* the doctrine that the bread and wine become the body and blood of Jesus. Lutherans affirm *consubstantiation,* the principle that the bread and wine are not changed into the body and blood of Jesus, but his body and blood are "in, with, and under" the bread and wine. Some Protestants explicitly reject both transubstantiation and consubstantiation and understand the meal as a memorial in which we remember Jesus and what he did.

But Jesus's death as a substitutionary atonement and questions about how he is present in the bread and wine (or simply remembered) were not issues in early Christianity. These questions were raised much, much later.

## Bread and Wine

In first-century Christian practice, a meal of bread and wine was accompanied by words associating them with the body and blood of Jesus. The synoptic Gospels and Paul report that Jesus on the night before he was betrayed, arrested, and executed spoke what are commonly called the "words of institution"—that he said some variation of "This is my body" as he broke a loaf of bread, and "This is my blood" as he poured wine into a cup.

The gist of these words could go back to Jesus. It is possible that he said something like this on the last night of his life. Or these words could be a post-Easter product; they could be the product of his first-century followers. But the historical verdict about whether the "words of institution" in some form go back to Jesus is not relevant to our focus. The relevant and important question is: What did this meal of bread and wine mean in its first-century historical context? It had several meanings.

First, bread and wine were the staple food and drink of the Mediterranean diet. Though a meal might include more than bread and wine, they were, and also symbolized, the material basis of existence. Moreover, early Christian sharing of bread and wine didn't consist of a wafer and a sip, but occurred in the context of a real meal, a full meal. It is worth thinking about the fact that the primary Christian sacrament could have been something else. But it is based on *food,* the sharing of the staff and stuff of life.

Second, the importance of shared meals in early Christianity was a continuation of the meal practice of Jesus. In his public activity, meals mattered, food mattered. Recall that the Lord's Prayer contains a petition for daily bread. Moreover, he was known (and sometimes criticized) for eating with people whom a respectable person would avoid: the marginalized, impure, and outcasts. Thus his meal practice also symbolized and embodied inclusivity in a world with sharp social boundaries.

It is thus ironic that many churches (including the church of my childhood) practiced "closed Communion." Most have now given it up. But until recently, one had to be a confirmed member of a denomination in order to receive Communion. But Jesus's meal practice was about openness—inclusivity.

A similar theme sounds in Paul. For Paul, the life of following Jesus is life "in Christ." We become "in Christ," "one with Christ," by acquiring a new identity and new way of being. This happens through dying and rising with Christ, symbolized in baptism. It also happens by ingesting Christ in this meal of bread and wine, which symbolize the body and blood of Jesus. We are united with Christ by sharing this meal—we become one body. Paul's image of the body of Christ is radically egalitarian; in Christ, there is no hierarchy of persons, whether Jew or Gentile, male or female, slave or free, and no hierarchy according to spiritual gifts (Gal. 3:28; 1 Cor. 12:12–27).

Third, there are overtly metaphorical uses of bread and wine. In John Jesus is "the bread of life," "the living bread that came down from heaven" (6:48, 51), the true manna in the wilderness. Jesus is food and drink. He satisfies our hunger and quenches our thirst. As manna in the wilderness, he is food for the journey. We are to eat lest the journey be too great for us. The theme of Jesus as bread in the wilderness also associates this meal with exodus imagery. Jesus, the gospel, and the kingdom of God are about a new exodus, a new liberation.

Fourth, the *body-and-blood* language intrinsically associates bread and wine with Jesus's death. In the New Testament, all four variations of the "words of institution" do so. Separation of body and blood occurs in a violent death. These words are thus reminders that Jesus died a violent death, killed by the powers that rule this world. This sacrament is about becoming one with this Jesus. It is about joining our lives to his life, our passion to his passion.

## THE EUCHARIST

Many eucharistic liturgies obscure these meanings, because their language reflects the framework of heaven-and-hell Christianity with its emphasis on sin, guilt, and substitutionary sacrifice. *Body* and *blood* highlight the fact that Jesus offered up his body and blood to atone for the sins of the world. The reason this language dominates the Eucharist is that most liturgies are the product of the last several hundred years, since the time when substitutionary sacrifice became widely accepted as the way to understand Jesus's death.

It is worthwhile noting that not all uses of the word *sacrifice* in the liturgy refer to substitutionary sacrifice. For example, in most liturgical churches, "Christ our Passover is sacrificed for us" is said during the Eucharist. The Passover lamb in Judaism was neither a substitutionary sacrifice nor a sacrifice for sin. In Exodus 12:13, the blood of the Passover lamb daubed on the doorposts of Hebrew homes is a signal for God's "angel of death" to pass over these homes. Then the Passover lamb is eaten; it is food for the journey out of Egypt and into a new life.

Nevertheless, in most eucharistic liturgies, substitutionary sacrifice is a major theme. In denominations that permit liturgical variety, the problem can be corrected more easily than in denominations that have a fixed and standard liturgy.

But even in these, all of the meanings from early Christianity can be brought to our understanding of the Eucharist today, whether our liturgies speak explicitly about them or not. The meanings of the Eucharist, this meal of bread and wine that goes back to Christian beginnings, are extraordinarily rich. The Eucharist is about food, shared food, and inclusivity; it is about becoming one with Christ and one in Christ; it is about spiritual food for the journey; and it is about participating in Jesus's passion for a different kind of world.

# CHAPTER 24

## The Lord's Prayer

What Protestants call the "Lord's Prayer" and Catholics the "Our Father" is the best-known prayer in the world. Included in almost every Christian worship service, it is also used in personal devotional practice. Most Christians know it by heart. Its words are so familiar as to be taken for granted. But its contents are surprising—for both what is included and what is not.[1]

We begin by setting it in its historical context. There are three versions of the Lord's Prayer in late first-century Christian documents, in Matthew, Luke, and the *Didache,* a writing from around 100 CE not included in the New Testament.

Matthew's version (6:9–13) is almost identical to the *Didache*'s. It is very familiar, as it is the form used in most churches:

> *Our Father in heaven,*
> *hallowed be your name.*
> *Your kingdom come.*
> *Your will be done,*
> *on earth as it is in heaven.*
> *Give us this day our daily bread.*

*And forgive us our debts,*
*as we also have forgiven our debtors.*
*And do not bring us to the time of trial,*
*but rescue us from the evil one [or from evil].*

Missing from Matthew is the concluding doxology used by Protestants but typically not by Catholics: "For the kingdom and the
power and the glory are yours forever." A form of this doxology is
included in the *Didache*'s version of the prayer.

Luke's version (11:2–4) is shorter and different in some ways:

*Father,*
*hallowed be your name.*
*Your kingdom come.*
*Give us each day our daily bread.*
*And forgive us our sins,*
*for we ourselves forgive everyone indebted to us.*
*And do not bring us to the time of trial.*

Because of the different versions, scholars are uncertain about
whether the prayer goes back to Jesus or whether the versions are
products of different Christian communities. If Jesus taught his
disciples to "memorize" this prayer, how do we account for the
different versions? Did he teach it in different ways, and the three
versions are accurate accounts of how he taught it on different
occasions? Or did he teach the core of it, and communities then
developed it in different ways?

But whether the prayer goes back to Jesus or is the composition
of his followers, it tells us the gist of what they thought mattered

most to him. To be committed to Jesus meant to pray for, to yearn for, what is in this prayer.

## What It Doesn't Include

What this prayer includes is very different from what the heaven-and-hell Christian framework emphasizes. To prepare for what it does include, we begin with what it doesn't include:

It's not about an afterlife. There is no petition asking God to take us to heaven when we die.

It's not about material success. There is no petition asking God to see that we "prosper"—an important point because of the prevalence of the prosperity gospel in some Christian churches today.

It's not about belief. It does not ask God to "help us to believe."

It's not about Jesus. Though the gist of it may go back to Jesus and thus tell us about his central concerns, there is nothing in it about believing in Jesus as the Son of God or that he died for our sins.

## What It Does Include

As we set the prayer in its first-century context, recall that those to whom Jesus spoke were primarily from the peasant class. We need to imagine what this prayer would have meant to the impoverished and disenfranchised.

*Our Father in heaven:* In the opening address to God, both Matthew and Luke use *Father.* Matthew's is the longer and familiar *Our Father in heaven.* In Luke, it is simply *Father.* Most likely, the Aramaic word *abba* lies behind the Greek word in Luke and probably in Matthew as well. *Abba* in Aramaic is a familiar form of "father," not a formal and distant one. It was commonly used to refer to one's own father and thus had the connotation of "papa" or "dear father" in English. The word was used by very young children, but also by adult children to refer to their own father. In both Judaism and early Christianity, it was also sometimes used for a beloved teacher, a "spiritual father," by students for their religious teacher. It is family imagery—about intimacy and belonging. *Abba* affirms that God is like a dear, intimate parent and that those who use this prayer belong to the same family.

*Hallowed be your name:* There are at least two ways of hearing this line. Are we reminding ourselves to *hallow* God's name, that is, to keep it holy by treating it reverently? Or is it addressed to God: "God, make your name holy"? Given that the rest of the prayer is addressed to God, the latter seems more likely. We will return to this near the end of this chapter.

*Your kingdom come:* The *kingdom* is, of course, the kingdom of God. It is the heart of Jesus's message in the synoptic Gospels. Indeed, in Mark, the coming of the kingdom of God is Mark's advance summary of the message of Jesus (1:15). Importantly, the kingdom of God is not about heaven, not about an afterlife. It is for the earth, as Matthew's longer version of the kingdom petition makes explicit: "Your will be done, *on earth* as it is in heaven." Scholar John Dominic Crossan makes this point in a particularly memorable way; he says, "Heaven's in great shape; earth is where the problems are."

So we pray for the coming of God's kingdom on earth. The kingdom of God is what life would be like on earth if God were king and the rulers of this world were not. The kingdom is God's passion for the earth: a world of economic justice and peace, where the nations beat their swords into plowshares and their spears into pruning hooks, every family has its own vine and fig tree (that is, its own land), and no one is made to live in fear (see Mic. 4:1–4; Isa. 2:2–4).

*Give us this day our daily bread:* The kingdom petition is followed immediately by the bread petition. *Bread* here means "food"—food for the day. For those of us who have plenty of food, the petition may sound like a reminder of our dependence on God and that we pray that God will continue to give us food. But recall that for the peasant class in the first century, food—enough food—was the primary survival issue. Many in that class lived at a subsistence level or worse, extremely vulnerable to lack of food for a variety of reasons: not enough money, unemployment, a bad crop year, or disease that made work impossible. The coming of the kingdom of God is about food—about the material basis of life for everybody. It is about bread for the world.

*Forgive us our debts, as we also have forgiven our debtors:* To say the obvious, this petition is about forgiveness. But of what? Some English translations use *debts,* others *sins,* and still others *trespasses.* Christians who attend worship services beyond their own denominations often need to wait to see which word will be used.

The difference between the English meanings of these words is significant. The use of the word *trespasses* can produce an odd result. It might make you think of a sign that says "No Trespassing" and sound like God is concerned that property rights not be violated. *Sins* suggests that the primary issue in our life with God is that we have sinned, and because we are forgiven, we should forgive those who have sinned against us. *Debts* suggests something quite different, unless we understand it as a metaphor for sins, as probably most people do. But it is not clear that we should hear it as an exact synonym for *sins*.

In Matthew and the *Didache,* the words used are Greek for *debts* and *debtors*. In Luke, the forgiveness petition uses the Greek word for *sin* in the first half ("forgive us our sins"), and the word for *debt* in the second half ("for we ourselves forgive everyone indebted to us").

Most likely the original wording was *debts* and *debtors*. Though they could in the first century have had the metaphorical meaning of *sins,* the fact that this petition follows the bread petition suggests that actual debts are meant. Along with acquiring enough food, debt was the main peril in peasant life. If a peasant family fell into debt, which would happen only if they were utterly desperate, failure to repay the debt could result in loss of their land (if they had any) or indentured servitude (temporary slavery) until the debt was repaid, even for the family as a whole. This petition asks God to forgive what we owe to God, as we forgive those who owe us. Consider that this, like the bread petition, follows the kingdom petition: the kingdom of God means daily food and debt forgiveness. Everybody is to have enough, and nobody is to be enslaved by economic misfortune. Debt forgiveness—whether taken literally or as a metaphor for release from economic impoverishment—is subversive of the way things are.

Is forgiveness of sins important? Of course. But to think that this petition is only about forgiving sins narrows and domesticates its meaning. Though forgiveness can have a radical meaning, as in connection with South Africa's Truth and Reconciliation Commission, it is often understood in a less radical way to mean something as common as "Let bygones be bygones," and then it is no longer subversive, but simply part of being a decent person.

*Do not bring us to the time of trial, but rescue us from evil:* For many Christians, this part of the prayer is more familiar as "Lead us not into temptation, but deliver us from evil." The phrases are general enough that scholars are uncertain if they had more specific meanings.

Luke and Matthew both have the first half of this part of the prayer, "Do not bring us to the time of trial." Some think this refers specifically to persecution: "Do not put us to the test of harassment, ostracism, maybe even violence." Some think its reference is more general: "Do not put us in a situation that tests our character, our loyalty, our allegiance." The Greek word is the same one used in the story of Jesus's "temptations" during his forty days in the wilderness (Matt. 4:1–11; Luke 4:1–13).

The second half, "rescue (or deliver) us from evil," can be understood in at least two ways. First, *evil* was often understood as a power that rules over us, dominates us, controls us. Thus the phrase may mean: "Deliver us from the power of evil." Second, the phrase could mean: "Deliver us from doing evil." Perhaps both are present; doing evil is often the product of being under the power of evil.

We return to the first petition: "Hallowed be your name." What does it mean to ask God to make God's name holy? The image is of God as "Father" and thus as the "householder" of the world. Because first-century society was patriarchal, the head of the household was spoken of as male. So, how does one judge whether a father, a householder, is a good householder? By how the household is run. Are children well taken care of? Does everybody get enough? Are some pampered and others neglected? How are the animals taken care of? The buildings? Is this household in good shape?

To ask God to make God's name holy is to ask God to make the world into a good household. It is parallel to and synonymous with the kingdom petition: "Your kingdom come . . . on earth, as it is in heaven."

The Lord's Prayer is a summary of what mattered most to Jesus. When we pray this prayer, we are praying for what he was passionate about. And because Jesus is the decisive revelation of God's passion, we are praying for what God is passionate about. We are praying for God's dream for the world. To pray this prayer is to be invited, enlisted, into participation in God's passion and the passion of Jesus.

# What's at Stake:
# The Heart of Christianity

How to understand Christian language is the central conflict in Christianity today. It not only divides American Christianity, but is also an issue elsewhere in the world. In the global Anglican communion, of which I am a member, a literal and absolute understanding of particular biblical texts threatens Anglican unity and could even lead to the expulsion of the American Episcopal church.

But the stakes are even higher than church unity. The issue is foundational: What is Christianity about? Is it, as heaven-and-hell Christianity implicitly or explicitly affirms, primarily about the afterlife and how we believe and behave now for the sake of heaven later? Is its central dynamic about sin, guilt, threat of punishment, and offer of pardon if we believe that Jesus died to pay the price for our sins? Is its relevance for this life absolute standards for personal righteousness and asking for forgiveness when we fail?

Heaven-and-hell Christianity is not simply a residue from the past, but continues in much of Christianity, sometimes unconsciously and sometimes consciously, especially among fundamentalist and conservative Christians. Of course, they also affirm that Christianity is about this life, that Christians are called to lead transformed lives. Nevertheless, for many the underlying question, spoken or unspoken, is our postmortem fate: "Where will you spend eternity?"

This form of Christianity is commonly individualistic, perhaps intrinsically so. It focuses on individuals; what matters is what we as individuals believe and do, for it is as individuals that we will one day go to heaven (or not). Its ethical teaching emphasizes issues of personal behavior. Consider the most publicly visible Christian moral conflicts today, the "family values" issues of abortion, contraception, sexual behavior and orientation, and the role of women in the church, family, and society.

Of course, individual conviction and behavior do matter. Christians are invited and called to a different way of seeing what is real, what life is about, and how then we should live. Conversion is intrinsically about individuals. But Christianity is not only about the conversion and transformation of individuals. It is about "the dream of God," God's passion for a transformed world here and now.

The world matters to God: the world of nature, for God loves the whole of creation, and the humanly created world, that is, whether its systems of politics, economics, and convention are just or unjust, fair or unfair, violent or nonviolent. God's passion is compassion—in our personal lives and also in our role in shaping the world. Christians are called to participate in God's passion for a different kind of world, a world of justice and peace.

Is this a utopian vision? Of course. It is impossible for me to imagine a world of perfect justice and peace. In this sense, utopia is "no place," one possible meaning of the Greek roots of the word. There will never be a world like that; it is an impossible dream.

But another possible meaning of its roots is "the good place," "the blessed place." Utopia is the ideal place, God's dream of the way things can be.

To realize that a utopian vision can never be achieved does not mean that we should cease seeking to embody it, however imperfectly. Rather, it calls us to participate in doing what we can to move toward that vision. Being Christian includes participating in God's passion for the world.

Heaven-and-hell Christianity with its focus on the afterlife and its individualism obscures the dream of God for this world. God's Word became flesh in Jesus not to take us out of this world, but to redeem this world. Recall that *redeem* means to liberate from slavery—to liberate the world from its bondage to the powers that obstruct God's dream of a transformed world.

## Two Visions of Christianity

These two visions of Christianity—one emphasizing the next world and what we must believe and do in order to get there, the other emphasizing God's passion for the transformation of this world—are very different. Yet they use the same language and share the same sacred scripture, the same Bible. What separates them is how the shared language is understood—whether within the framework of heaven-and-hell Christianity or within the framework of God's passion for transformation in this world.

The latter framework, I am convinced, is more biblical, ancient, and traditional (even as it is not conventional, but subversive). It takes seriously the ancient meanings of Christian language in ancient context. The former is the product of a process that began when Christianity became allied with dominant culture, initially in the Roman Empire in the fourth century and then gradually in all of Europe and parts of the Middle East. The result was that Christianity became largely a religion of the afterlife and the post-mortem fate of us as individuals. It was no longer about changing the way the world is, for the world was now ruled by Christian authorities. Heaven-and-hell Christianity domesticates—indeed, commonly eliminates—the political passion of the Bible.

How we speak and understand Christian language matters. It can change and revitalize our understanding of what Christianity is about. It also matters for those Christians for whom its conventional meanings have become so problematic that some have stopped using biblical and Christian language. But if we avoid the language of our faith because of uncertainty about what it means, we grant a monopoly on it to those who are most certain about its meaning. That would be unfortunate, for the language is extraordinarily rich, wise, and transformative.

Moreover, if we neglect or reject biblical and Christian language because of its common meanings, a serious question arises: Can we be Christian without using the language of Christianity? If this book's premise that religions are like languages is correct, the answer is no. Being Christian includes "speaking Christian."

Not being Christian is not a sentence of doom. Can people love God without being Christian? Yes. Can people be passionate about the dream of a world of justice and peace without being Christian? Yes. Some in other religious traditions share this vision. Some atheists do too. The central ethical passion of the Bible is affirmed beyond Christianity. So the question isn't whether one must be Christian in order to love God or to share this passion.

Rather, the question is whether we can be Christian without sharing God's passion for transformation of ourselves and the world. Can we be Christian without embracing God's passion for a world of compassion, justice, and peace?

This is an especially important and difficult question for contemporary American Christians. As both an American and a Christian, I am dismayed by much of what I see in American Christianity. Statistically, we are the most Christian country in the world. When asked what religion they are, about 80 percent of Americans respond "Christian." True, only about half of these are actively involved in a church, but that's still a very big number. And the United States is the imperial power of our time, even as some worry that our power is waning. To speak of the United States as an empire not so long ago was a left-wing claim. But now conservatives declare it as well and celebrate it.

The combination of being Christian and American creates a very ambiguous situation. We are the most Christian country in the world—and yet we are the world's greatest military power. With 5 percent of the world's population, we account for about half of the world's military spending. We have over 700 military bases in about 130 countries. Our navy is as powerful as the next thirteen navies of the world combined. Not surprisingly, the United States Air Force is the most powerful in the world. More surprising is the second most powerful air force: the United States Navy. As a country, we are determined to be as militarily powerful as the rest of the world put together. Though our national motto is "In God We Trust," clearly what we really trust in is power, especially military power.

We are the most Christian nation in the world—and yet we have the greatest income inequality of any of the developed nations to whom we typically compare ourselves. Our income inequality is—literally—almost off the charts. On the graphs portraying it in relation to that of other industrial nations, we are almost an outlier. Moreover, income inequality in America has been growing for about thirty years. The wealthy have become more wealthy and powerful, and the middle and lower economic classes have seen their well-being decline—in the most Christian country on the globe.

And yet at least a slight majority of American Christians endorse a foreign policy that depends upon overwhelming military power and a domestic policy that emphasizes less government and lower taxes. Wittingly or unwittingly, this favors the wealthy, especially the top 1 to 2 percent of our population, at the expense of everybody else.

Thus the stakes are high for American Christians. What is at stake in reclaiming Christian language is the future of Christianity as well as the future of our country. Are we as a nation to become more and more like the domination systems of the ancient and not so distant past, all of which have passed into history? Or might we, as the most Christian nation in the world, change our course and become committed to compassion, justice, and peace?

It may be too much to expect. The record of past imperial powers is not encouraging. They're all gone. The major voices of the Bible name the reason: they became filled with *hubris,* a Greek word that is most often translated into English as "pride." As mentioned earlier, *hubris* means more than "pride" commonly does. It is okay to feel good about yourself, to be proud, when you have done something really good. But *hubris* is more than this; it means puffing up beyond appropriate size—one's self, or one's country, or even one's religion. *Hubris* is ultimately about idolatry—making something other than God the center of one's life and security and vision. *Hubris* is the classic imperial sin—and it has always led to imperial downfall.

We need not be too dismayed about this, even as it is morally and practically important that our country change our course. When an empire falls, the homeland often is still all right. Of course, there are exceptions. Sometimes the fall of an empire leads to desolation, but not always. The British Empire is gone, but the United Kingdom is doing okay. So also the French Empire and the Ottoman Empire, but France and Turkey are all right. The demise of the American Empire—our reducing ourselves to appropriate size—might be a good thing.

## What Christianity's All About

Christians have often made being Christian very complicated, especially those forms that emphasize believing the right beliefs. Infant baptism or adult baptism? Predestination or free will? Does the Holy Spirit proceed from "the Father only" or from "the Father and the Son," an issue that led to the split between Western and Eastern Christianity in 1054? Infralapsarianism or supralapsarianism—did God decide to send Jesus as the Messiah before or after the fall, a conflict that divided the Dutch Reformed Church in the early 1600s? Does the bread and wine of the Eucharist become the body and blood of Jesus, or is the Eucharist about remembering the last supper of Jesus? Does being Christian mean affirming the "five fundamentals," including biblical inerrancy and a literal understanding of the virginal conception of Jesus and his physical and bodily resurrection? When Christianity is about "correct beliefs," it does become complex.

But ultimately, the central message of Christianity is simple. It is about loving God and loving what God loves. That means loving God as disclosed in the Bible and most decisively revealed in Jesus.

Jesus is the incarnation, the embodiment, of what can be seen of God's character and passion in a life lived among us. His passion was the kingdom of God—what life would be like on a transformed earth. The world is God's passion.

Christianity is a magnificent tradition. Like all religious and human traditions, it has its shadow side. But at its best, it is about truth, goodness, and beauty. And it addresses the two great human yearnings—our longing for personal transformation and our desire that the world be a better place. The Christian message reduced to its essentials is: love God (as known in Jesus) and change the world.

Claiming this vision involves reclaiming Christian language. How we understand "speaking Christian" matters.

# Acknowledgments

I n the first half of the year that it took me to write this book, my one remaining sibling—once upon a time there were four of us—began a steep decline and died. I was fortunate that Beverly lived only three hours away and grateful that I could be with her for a day or two. sometimes more, weekly. She died in March, and I became the executor of her estate, something I had not done before. Her decline and death delayed my completion of this book.

And so I am also grateful to my long-term partners and colleagues at HarperOne, Mickey Maudlin and Mark Tauber. With generous patience and not a hint of strict parent, they graciously extended the manuscript deadline more than once.

I am also grateful to all of the people, living and dead, scholars and nonscholars, for what I have learned about Christian language and "speaking Christian" since I first became aware about fifty years ago that this language might mean something different than I thought. They are too numerous to mention. I understand, but do not wish to emulate the effort of some who win awards to hurriedly mention everybody to whom they are indebted before the producer tells the musicians to start playing.

I also wish to thank Lisa Zuniga, Ann Moru, Carol Lastrucci, Joseph Rutt, and Claudia Boutote.

# Notes

CHAPTER 1: SPEAKING CHRISTIAN

1. George Lindbeck, *The Nature of Doctrine* (Philadelphia: Westminster, 1984).
2. "Jesus, Reconsidered: Book Sparks Evangelical Debate," interview on NPR's "Morning Edition," March 26, 2010. (Interviewer was Barbara Bradley Hagerty.)
3. Gretta Vosper, *With or Without God: Why the Way We Live Is More Important Than What We Believe* (Toronto: HarperCollins, 2008).

CHAPTER 2: BEYOND LITERALISM

1. David Tracy, *The Analogical Imagination* (New York: Crossroad, 1987; first published in 1981).

CHAPTER 3: SALVATION

1. Pew Forum on Religion and Public Life, "Many Americans Say Other Faiths Can Lead to Eternal Life," reported on December 18, 2008.
2. *The American Heritage College Dictionary,* fourth ed. (Boston, New York: Houghton Mifflin, 2004); *The Random House Webster's College Dictionary* (New York: Random House, 2001); *The Concise Oxford American Dictionary* (New York: Oxford Univ. Press, 2006).
3. I have not checked the English translations most widely used in evangelical and Catholic churches, but the number would not be much different. Word counts do not include texts from the Apocrypha.
4. Dan. 12:2–3. "Many of those who sleep in the dust of the earth shall awake, some to everlasting life, and some to shame and everlasting contempt. Those who are wise shall shine like the brightness of the sky, and those who lead many to righteousness, like the stars forever and ever."
5. Walter Brueggemann, *The Bible Makes Sense* (Atlanta: John Knox, 1977), esp. chap. 3.
6. 1 Sam. 8:4–22, 10:17–19. These chapters also contain a pro-monarchy narrative (9:1–10:16), reflecting the ambivalence in ancient Israel about the monarchy.
7. Verna J. Dozier, *The Dream of God* (Cambridge: Cowley, 1991); Desmond Tutu uses the notion in the titles of two of his recent books: *God Has a Dream* and *God's Dream.*

CHAPTER 4: THE BIBLE
1. Vosper, *With or Without God*, p. 53 and elsewhere.


CHAPTER 5: GOD
1. Karen Armstrong, *A History of God* (New York: Knopf, 1994); *The Case for God* (New York: Knopf, 2009).
2. For modern theological expressions of this distinction, see Paul Tillich, *The Courage to Be* (New Haven: Yale Univ. Press, 1952), pp. 182–90; John A. T. Robinson, *Honest to God* (Philadelphia: Westminster, 1963), esp. chaps. 2 and 3.
3. William James, *The Varieties of Religious Experience* (New York: Collier, 1961; first published in 1902), pp. 394–402.


CHAPTER 6: GOD'S CHARACTER
1. See H. Richard Niebuhr, *The Responsible Self* (San Francisco: Harper & Row, 1963), pp. 98–107.
2. Sam Keen, *The Passionate Life* (San Francisco: Harper & Row, 1983), pp. 112–14.


CHAPTER 9: EASTER
1. In Paul Copan, ed., *Will the Real Jesus Please Stand Up?* (Grand Rapids: Baker, 1998), pp. 117–28.


CHAPTER 10: BELIEVING AND FAITH
1. Wilfrid Cantwell Smith, *Belief and History* (Charlottesville: Univ. Press of Virginia, 1977) and *Faith and Belief: The Difference Between Them* (Oxford: Oneworld, 1998; first published in 1979).


CHAPTER 11: MERCY
1. A central theme in Abraham Heschel, *The Prophets* (New York: Harper & Row, 1962).


CHAPTER 14: FORGIVENESS AND REPENTANCE
1. "You Are Accepted," a sermon in Tillich's *The Shaking of the Foundations* (Gloucester, MA: Peter Smith Publisher, Inc., 1988).


CHAPTER 20: THE RAPTURE AND THE SECOND COMING
1. For an excellent and very readable book that describes how belief in the rapture emerged, the effects of that belief, and an alternative and far more persuasive way of reading the biblical texts that are foundational to "rapture theology," see Barbara Rossing, *The Rapture Exposed* (Boulder, CO: Westview Press, 2004).


CHAPTER 21: HEAVEN
1. See Rita Nakashima Brock and Rebecca Parker, *Saving Paradise* (Boston: Beacon, 2008).

CHAPTER 22: THE CREEDS AND THE TRINITY

1. See, for example, Luke Timothy Johnson, *The Creed* (New York: Doubleday, 2003); Berard L. Marthaler, *The Creed,* rev. ed. (New London, CT: Twenty-Third Publications, 2007); and on The Apostles Creed but with relevance to the Nicene Creed, Joan Chittister, *In Search of Belief* (Liguori, MO: Liguori/Triumph, 1999).

2. All English versions of the Nicene Creed are, of course, translations. The version printed here was produced by an ecumenical consulting group in the mid-1970s and is widely used in American churches.

CHAPTER 24: THE LORD'S PRAYER

1. On the Lord's Prayer, see especially John Dominic Crossan, *The Greatest Prayer: Rediscovering the Revolutionary Message of the Lord's Prayer* (San Francisco: HarperOne, 2010).

# Discussion Questions

These questions can be used by individual readers and also in reading groups in which participants are invited to share their memories and thoughts. Many of them invite reflection on previous or current understandings and are best used before treating the content of the relevant chapter. Some invite reflection about material in a particular chapter.

1. How important has the promise of heaven (and perhaps the threat of hell) been to the forms of Christianity that you have experienced or heard about?

2. How central were sin and forgiveness to your end-of-childhood impression of Christianity? How central are they to the forms of Christianity that you're now familiar with?

3. Consider the words *salvation, sacrifice, redemption, righteousness, repentance,* and *mercy.* How would you define each? How do you think Christians usually define these words? Is there a difference? The book says: "We need to ask afresh: What does this language mean? What does it mean to use these words?" (p. 19). How do you think reclaiming these words will help?

4. How does the framework of heaven-and-hell Christianity affect the way people interpret the Bible? Why do you think the church focuses so much on the afterlife, when the Bible mostly focuses on life here on earth?

5. Has a literal interpretation of biblical and Christian language been part of your experience? Has literalism affected you? If so, in what ways? Do you think the movement toward literalization has distorted the meaning of the Bible? If so, how? Can you think of examples of when you have encountered literalization?

6. "A historical approach is greatly illuminating. Language comes alive in its context. Moreover, a historical approach prevents us from projecting modern and often misleading meanings back

into the past. It is a way of escaping the provinciality of the present. It recognizes that the Bible was not written to us or for us, but within and for ancient communities" (p. 28). How does a historical approach act as an accountability structure for reading the Bible? What does it mean when the book says that the Bible was not written to us or for us? It also argues that the best way to interpret the Bible is through the "historical-metaphorical" approach. Do you agree with this model? Why or why not?

7. According to the book, the Bible is a human product, not a divine one. How does this shape your understanding of what's written in the Bible?

8. "The Bible includes [our spiritual ancestors'] experiences of God, their stories about God, their understandings of life with God, and how we should live. But it is their story—*not* God's infallible, inerrant, and absolute story. . . . Did God ever command that all the men, women, and children of our enemies be killed? Did God ever say that slavery was okay? Did God ever forbid remarriage after divorce? Did God ever command that adulterers be stoned? That children who dishonor their parents should be killed? That women should be silent in church? That same-sex relationships are an abomination? That God is violent? That Jesus is coming soon, and that his second coming will involve incredible suffering and death for most of humanity—indeed, the destruction of the world itself?" (pp. 58–59). How do you react when you encounter these kinds of teachings in the Bible? How do you determine which teachings to pay attention to?

9. What are your earliest memories associated with Jesus? By the end of childhood, how did you think of him? Who did you think he was? Why did he matter? How would you describe who he is now? What caused your views to change?

10. What memories do you have of the death of Jesus from earlier in your life? If you grew up in a church that observed Lent and Holy Week, what impression did you get of what they were about? Has your perception of the death of Jesus changed?

11. When you were young, what did you think Easter was about—what happened and why it mattered? What do you understand it to mean now? What do you think it means to most Christians?

12. In ordinary English, what do you think of when you hear the word *believe*? When do you hear it being used? When do you use it yourself? What are its immediate associations? What changes when you think of it primarily as *trust* and *belove*?

13. When you hear the words *mercy* and *merciful,* what do you think of? What are the associations, meanings, resonances of these words? In a church context? In secular usage?

14. What are your associations with the word *righteous*? When somebody says about a person, "He's very righteous," what do you think is being said? When you hear, "God is a righteous God," what do you think is meant? How would you describe what we should mean by the word today?

15. What are your associations with the word *sin*? If you grew up Christian, was sin emphasized in your church? Your family? Your own mind? If so, what did you think it meant? What does it mean to you now? What changes if we expand our understanding of the human problem from just sin to also include other biblical categories such as bondage, exile, infirmity, blindness, and so on?

16. What role has the word *forgiveness* played in your life? Share the most profound story of forgiveness you have ever heard. What does forgiveness mean to you? What does it imply? When you think of being "forgiven by God," what do you think of? When you think of forgiveness as something we should practice in our lives, what do you think it means? How often have you felt the need to forgive someone or to be forgiven by someone?

17. Was the term *born again* part of your childhood experience? If so, what did you think it meant? What are your associations with the term now? What do you think it means in common usage? Ideally, what might it look like for you to be born again in a historical-metaphorical sense?

18. In John 14:6, Jesus declares: "I am the way, and the truth, and the life. No one comes to the Father except through me." What has this

verse meant to you at an earlier time? What does it mean to you now? Do you think Christianity should proclaim that Jesus is the only way to salvation? If Christianity sees itself as one faith among many, what do we say is distinctive or true about Christianity?

19. That Jesus "ascended into heaven" is in the New Testament and in two ancient Christian creeds commonly used in worship services. What have you thought or wondered about the ascension of Jesus? What has it meant to you? What might it mean when we think of it as the reign of the post-Easter Jesus who sits at the right hand of God?

20. At Pentecost the Holy Spirit came upon the early Christians, and they spoke in a language understood by people from multiple cultures and nations. What might it mean today for us to experience Pentecost?

21. Have you heard of the *rapture* in which "true believers" are taken to heaven and the rest are left behind to face the trials and tribulations of the final seven years before the second coming and last judgment? If so, what have you thought of it? What might be a more hopeful and powerful understanding of the return of Jesus?

22. What are your associations with *heaven*? When you hear the word, what do you think of? How important is heaven to your understanding of Christianity? Some describe themselves as "agnostics" about the afterlife; they think we cannot know what will happen upon death. What happens to your view of Christianity if you discover heaven to be a vague and ambiguous concept in the Bible that may not promise an afterlife?

23. Have you had difficulty saying the creed? If so, why? What parts have been most puzzling or troublesome?

24. What memories do you have of the Eucharist, Mass, Communion, or the Lord's Supper, as it is variously called? What did you think it was about? How does its practice change for you if you see it primarily as a celebration of inclusion and as sustenance for our journey on earth?

25. Has your interpretation of the Bible changed after reading this book? In what ways? Are you now more likely or less likely to use classic Christian terms and phrases?